GUARDIOLA-KLOPP-POCHETTINO-SARRI

OFFENSIVE TACTICS

TACTICAL ANALYSIS AND TRAINING SESSIONS

LUCAS RIVAS

OFFENSIVE TACTICS / Lucas Rivas - 1st edition
LIBROFUTBOL.com, 2021.

160 pages; 15,2 x 22,9 cm.

ISBN 978-987-8370-71-2

1. Fútbol.
CDD 796.3342

OFFENSIVE TACTICS
from Lucas Rivas

Cover and layout:
Luciano Medvetkin

Photo's autor: © Lucas Rivas

ISBN 978-987-8370-71-2 | **FIRST EDITION: NOVEMBER 2021**

ediciones@librofutbol.com
+54 9 11 2215 1982
librofutbol

Olga Cossettini 1112 - office 8F - Ciudad de Buenos Aires - Argentina

Índice

STEP ONE

Go to Google Play or the Apple Store and download the QR App Reader

STEP TWO

Install and open the App on your mobile device

STEP THREE

Scan the QR code to access exclusive content

Introduction

In this book I want to show you the patterns of play that are identified with each coach, and the possible solutions for each scenario that the opponent may pose. From how the game is managed from a goal kick (dead ball), to how to progress and finish each play.

In the offensive phase, we will analyze attacks where these teams break through the defense even when the opponent is well organized. Everything will be evaluated from a tactical and strategic point of view, trying to decipher what the coaches want from their teams in the face of their opponent's specific plans.

For each coach, we have analyzed eight specific plays in detail. Three of these will be buildouts from goal kicks and five will be combinations of progression and finishing.

The first part will be divided into goal kicks where the team can initiate play and progress from their own goal from a dead ball situation, with the opponent either pressuring or waiting, depending on the situation.

In the second part we will analyze progression and finishing. What are the concepts that allow these coaches' teams to be able to finish their attacks? What do they do to break down organized defenses? What concepts do they use most frequently? What just happened, and why did it just happen?

Finally, we will move forward with a deep analysis to review each concept in minute detail in order to help you, the reader, understand the motives of each action and to be able to apply them with your own teams.

All good analysis must involve a practical component. Therefore, we will have 33 exercises; 11 training sessions dedicated exclusively to the concepts we have analyzed. We will try to extract, directly from the analysis, those situations that simulate these actions. Because coaches are the "facilitators of the context", we must get the players to recreate the situations that we want, and that we think will happen during competition.

Lucas Rivas
The Author

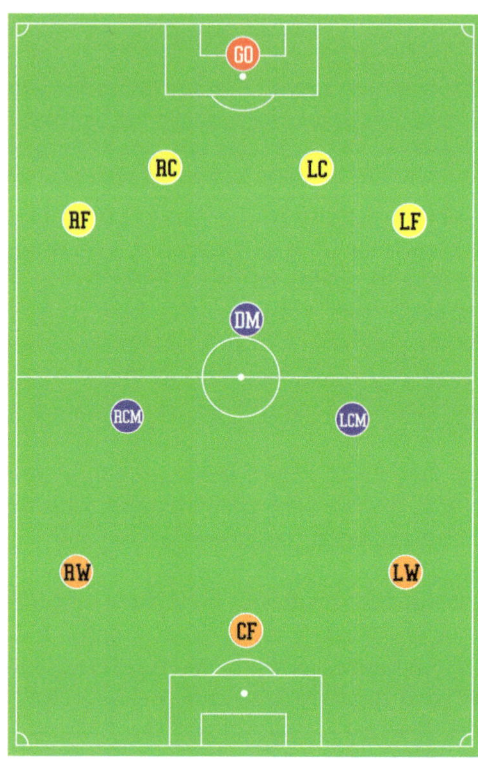

GO Goalkeeper
RF Right fullback
RC Right centerback
LC Left centerback
LF Left fullback
RCM Right center midfielder
DM Defensive midfielder
LCM Left center midfielder
RW Right winger
CD Center forward
EI Left winger

- GO Goalkeeper
- RF Right fullback
- RC Right centerback
- LC Left centerback
- LF Left fullback
- RCM Right center midfielder
- LCM Left center midfielder
- RW Right winger
- AM Attacking midfielder
- LW Left winger
- CF Center forward

CHAPTER 1

PEP GUARDIOLA

INTRODUCTION

Usual system of play. Used in 77% of the games.

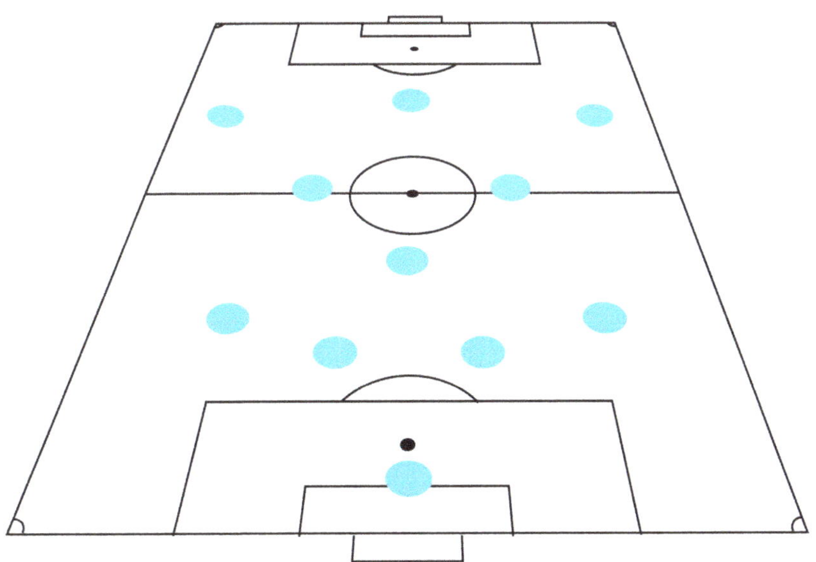

1-4-3-3

Key points of guardiola's attacking organization

- Prioritize arriving to the middle of the field with the ball under control
- Superiorities
- Rapid circulation of the ball
- Use of the third man
- Dismarking
- Perception and interpretation
- Individual qualities

BUILDING OUT THROUGH THE GOAL KICK

Situation 1: building out through the centerback - under pressure - superiorities

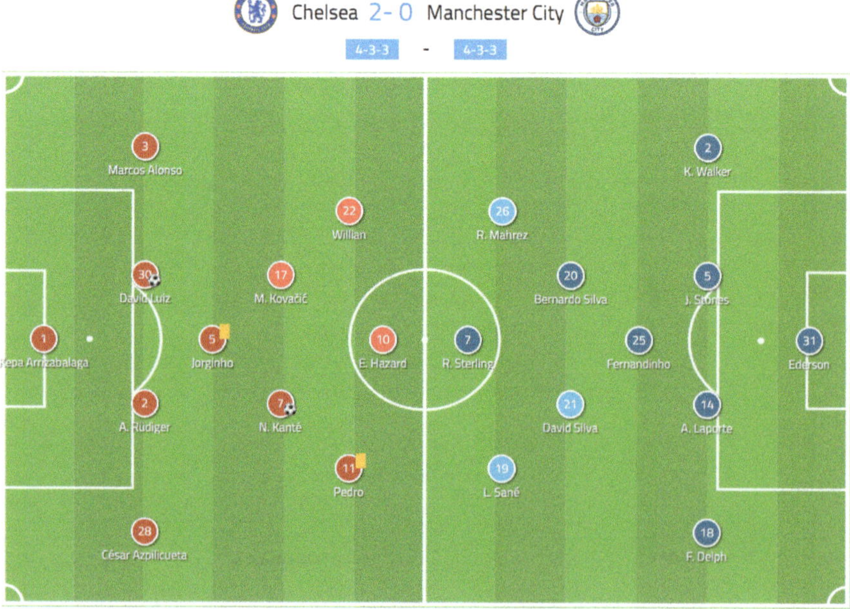

Analyzing the situation

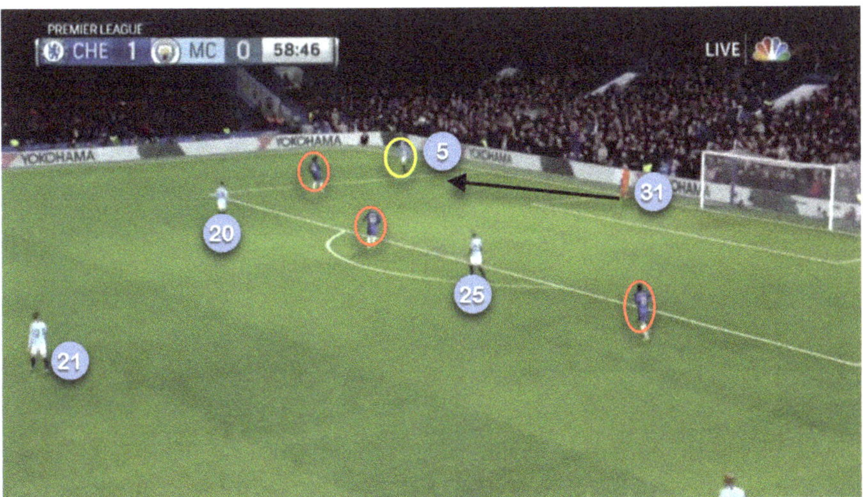

The first thing we see is a numerical superiority in favor of Manchester City. The three Chelsea forwards take up intermediate positions, with the objective of being able to press once City puts the ball into play.

Ederson (31) plays short to John Stones (5), who receives pressure from the opposing left winger, who leaves his marking reference (the right fullback, Walker) to his team mate (the left center midfielder). He does this in a way that blocks the passing line to the central right midfielder (20).

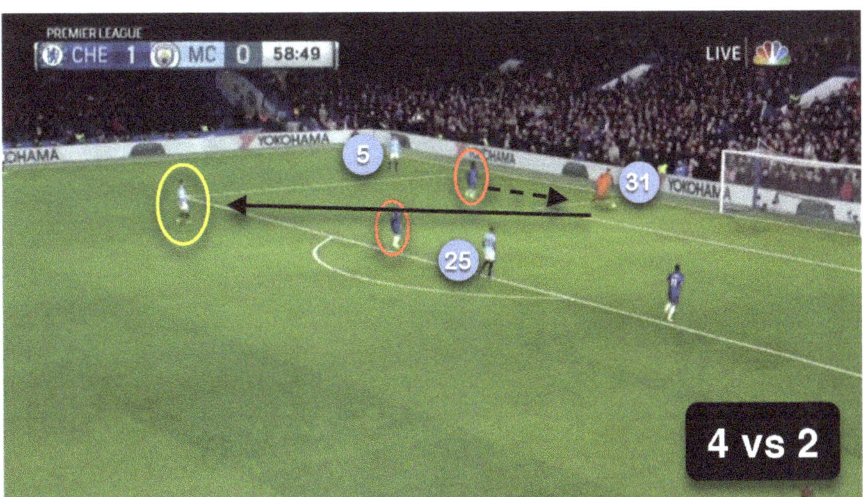

Stones (5) plays ball back to the goalkeeper (31), Willian (the left forward) continues to press, this time blocking the passing line to the central defender (5) who made the pass, with the intention of preventing the ball from being returned. The interior midfielder (20), now free, becomes an option to receive the ball and break this first line of pressure. Ederson (31) sees and executes the pass.

Bernardo Silva (20) takes an oriented touch forward and is pressured by the left center midfielder, who is in an intermediate marking position between the right fullback and the interior midfielder who has the ball. This is a situation of 2v1 numerical superiority. Bernardo Silva plays to the fullback, eliminating the opposing pressure. Kyle Walker runs with the ball into the midfield, where he is fouled.

Situation 2: buildout through the centerback without initial pressure

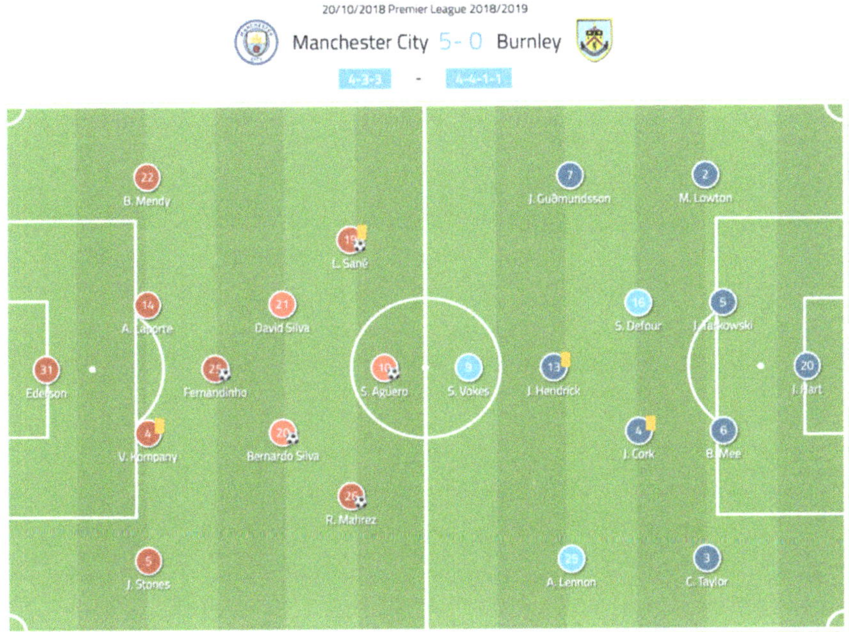

Analyzing the situation

The positioning of Manchester City forces Burnley to separate their lines. City generally opens up their centerbacks (4 and 14) and fullbacks (5 and 22), with Fernandinho (25) located at the edge of the penalty area, close to his central midfielders (20 and 21). The three forwards are left far up the field in the opponent's half, knowing that there is no offside on a goal kick. This stretches out the opponent. Guardiola's team has created an 8v6 superiority in the build out. The goalkeeper Ederson (31) decides to play with the left centerback (14).

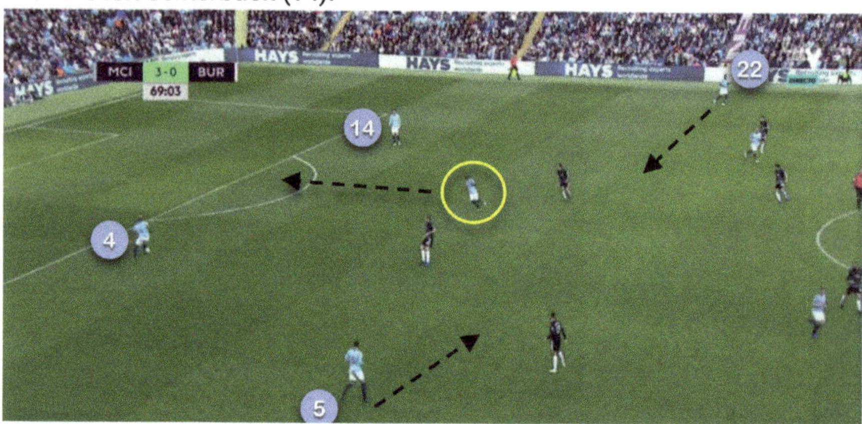

Burnley decides not to press and drops back, while maintaining their organization. Aymeric Laporte (14) passes to Vincent Kompany (4). Fernandinho (25) drops back to insert himself between the two centerbacks and generate a 3 v 2, allowing the centerbacks the possibility of opening themselves up and widening the field.

The fullbacks, John Stones (5) and Benjamin Mendy (22) move towards the middle of the field (to a center midfield position), forcing the opponent's wingers to move in and the center midfielders to stay back. In addition to becoming passing options, this pins the opponents in the middle of the field

and frees up the wings. Kevin De Bruyne (17), the right center midfielder, positions himself in the wide right channel to become a passing option. De Bruyne had entered the game in the 58th minute, replacing right center midfielder Bernardo Silva.

Fernandinho (25), plays the ball to Kompany (4) in a 3v2 numerical superiority with Stones (5), who appears behind the opposing line of pressure. Kompany takes a touch, passes, and looks for a wall pass, which eliminates the first line of pressure.

Kompany receives the wall pass from stones and launches a pass that breaks lines between the outside left midfielder and center midfielder of the

opponent. The ball is directed to City's right winger (26), who has moved into the middle of the field. De Bruyne (17) starts a run down the wing to become a passing option. David Silva (21), Kun Agüero (10) and Leroy Sané (19) accompany him, maintaining the width of the field.

Situation 3: build out through the long pass – The opponent defends 1 v 1

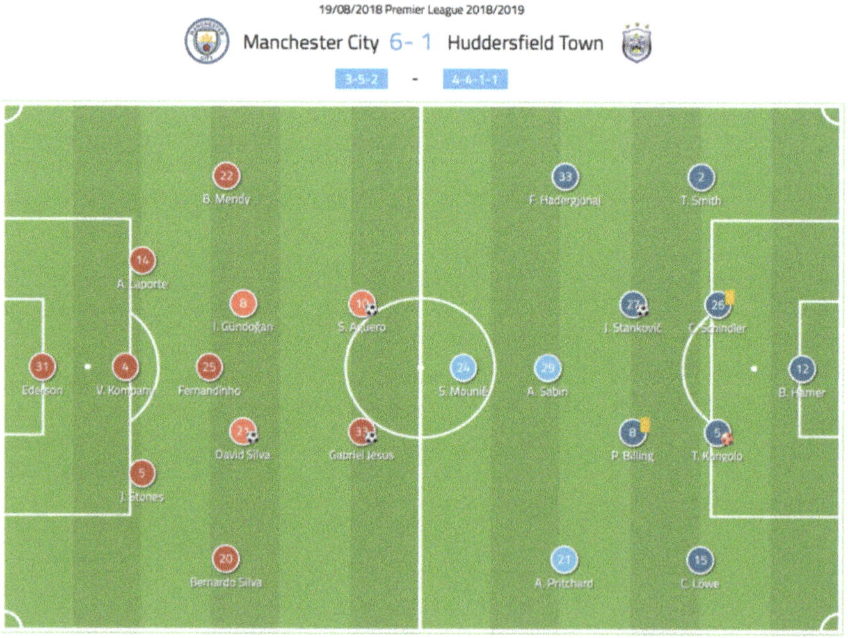

Analyzing the situation

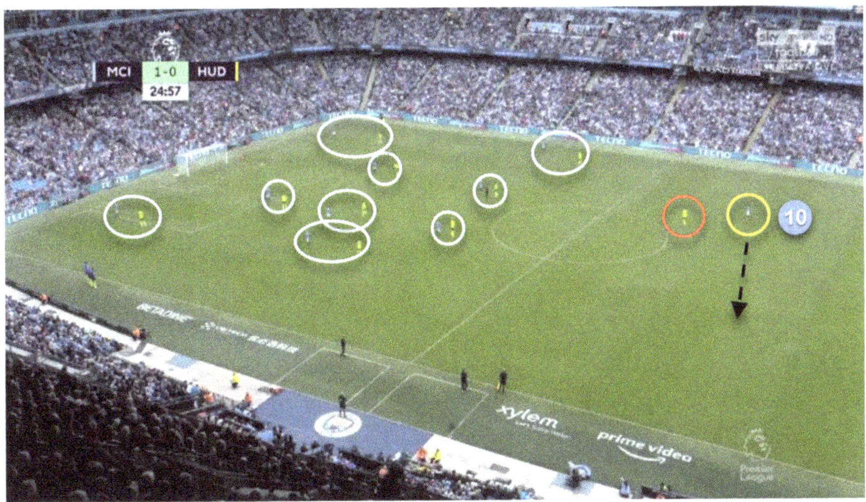

Huddersfield attempts to play man-on-man during City's buildout. Guardiola, evaluating that his opponent is not going to let him play out of the back comfortably through his defenders, decides to position all of his players in their own half of the field except for Agüero (10).

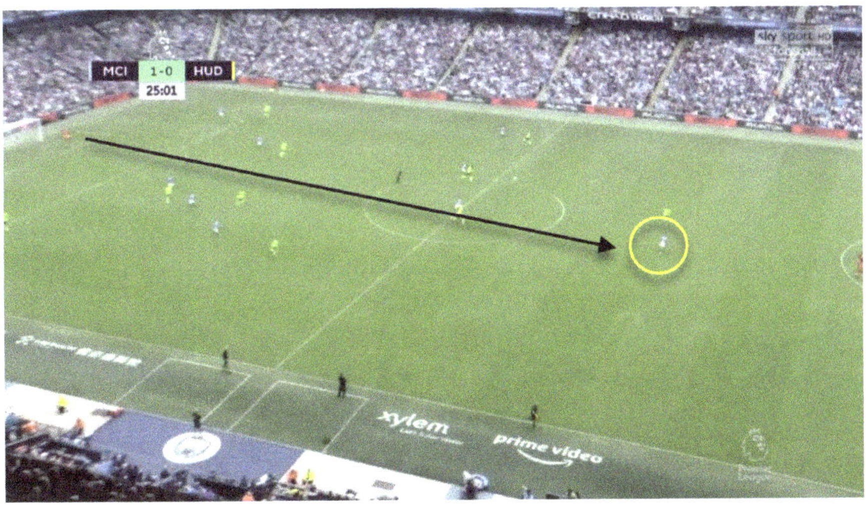

Manchester City is playing with a 3-5-2 system against a 4-4-1-1. Kun remains in the opposing half of the field, behind the back of the player who is marking him, knowing that there is no offside on a goal kick. The goalkeeper launches the ball at the exact moment Agüero starts his sprint towards the opponent's goal. Kun starts his run when he observes that his marker has looked away.

THE RUN DICTATES THE PASS

The receiver will show where the pass should be played by starting their movement into the space where they want to receive it (dismark). The player who is going to receive the ball knows the right time and place to dismark. This concept can be transferred to any position or game situation.

PROGRESSION - FINISHING

Guardiola: "In the final quarter of the field, I leave my players free to resolve the situation however they want, but they have to arrive to that zone of the field".

Situation 1: playing between the lines. Fullback - center midfield relationship

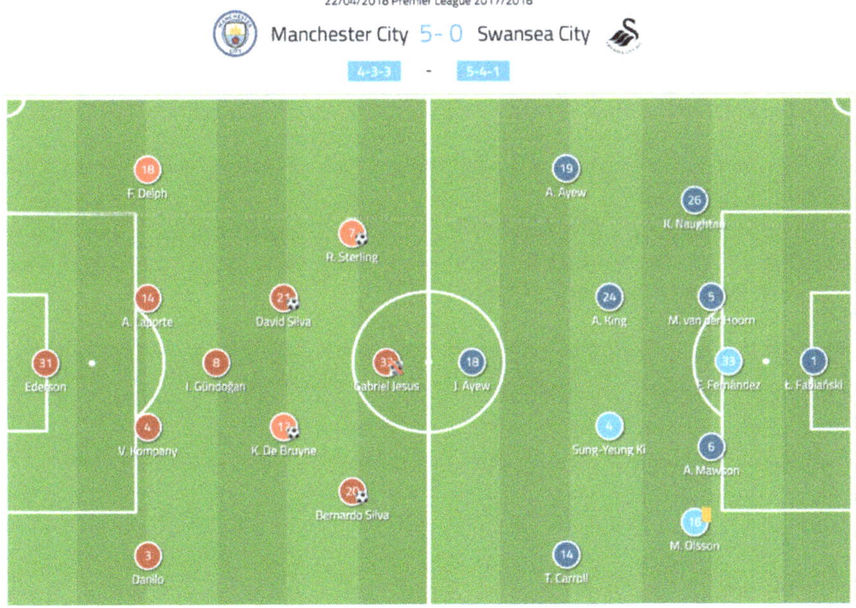

Analyzing the situation

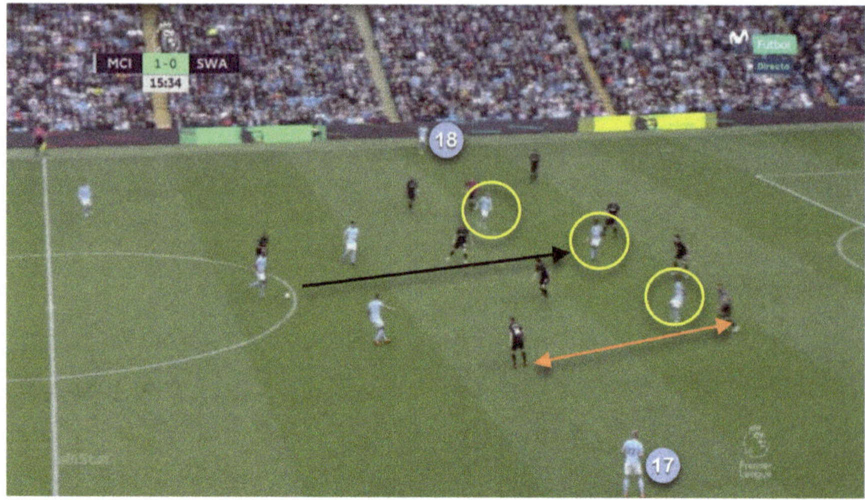

The central defender, Kompany, enters the opposing half with the ball, with time and space.

Players can be observed between the lines and in width. It can also be observed that the opponent has compressed, forming a "compact" team between the midfield and defensive lines.

Kompany passes inside to Sterling, who finds himslef in the central zone. Sterling, who has little time or space, plays first time to David Silva, who plays the ball into space to the left fullback who is out wide.

Delph tries to get in behind but encounters an opponent, while Silva, always active, goes to give support. They carry out a wall pass, which allows Delph to eliminate his marker with just a "give and go".

Delph looks up and plays a pass to Sterling, who enters the six yard box unmarked and converts the chance.

WHY HAVE PLAYERS BETWEEN THE LINES IN THE OPPONENT'S HALF OF THE FIELD?

This forces the players in the last line to shorten their distances to the midfielders, which generates more space between themselves and the goalkeeper.
If they don't do this, the opponents who have overcome the midfield line when they receive the ball will be able to control, turn, and play one versus one against the last line of defenders.
Players between the lines in the central channel force the opposing team to close down the spaces within the lines (between players in the same line), which generates space on the wings.

Situation 2: play short to attract. Patience. Generating space.

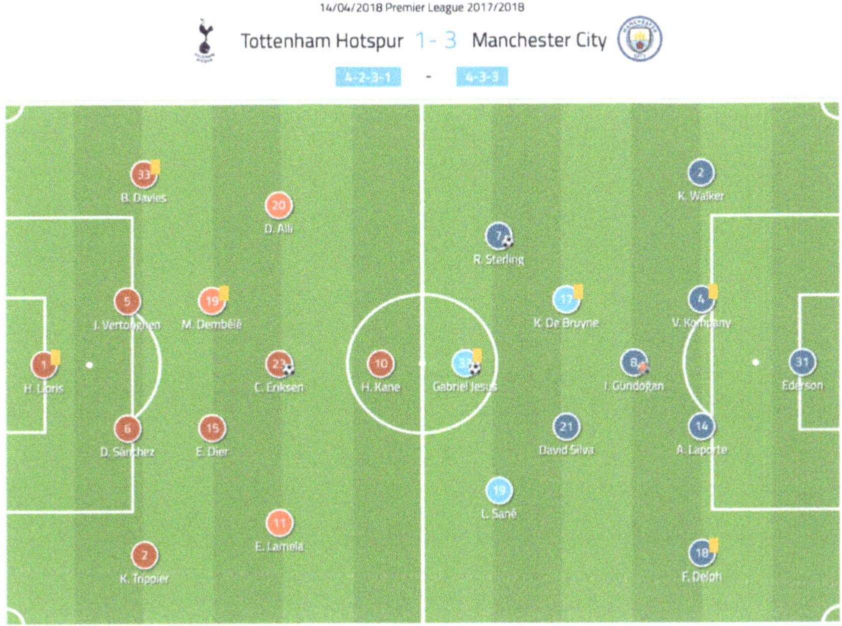

Analyzing the situation

The situation starts with Manchester City in possession with time and space, carrying out short passes while the opposing team is compact in their own half. City passes the ball from side to side to move Tottenham's defensive structure and find space to progress.

Tottenham exerts pressure when the ball reaches the wings, so City decides to play back in order to maintain possession, all the way back to Ederson in goal. This prompts Tottenham to move their lines forward into the opposing half with the intent to press and recover the ball.

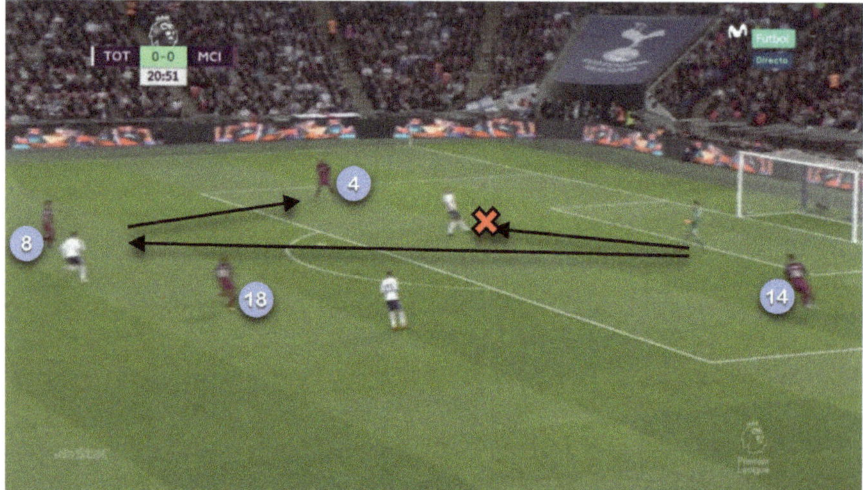

The concept of the third man is used to break the opponent's press. Ederson cannot play to Kompany, because that passing line is blocked. In order to be able to play to him, a third player needs to come and create a passing line.

Kompany runs forward with the ball and plays a long pass in front of the dismarking Gabriel Jesús, leaving all of the opposing players behind.

PATIENCE

Patience is one of the keys to Guardiola's teams. Be patient in order to control the game and not lose the ball. Find the correct moment, space, and pass to break the opposition lines, and disorganize your opponent. Patience will be reflected in the concept of playing short to attract and playing long to find space.

Situation 3: playing quickly to the opposite side. Dismarking by the 9

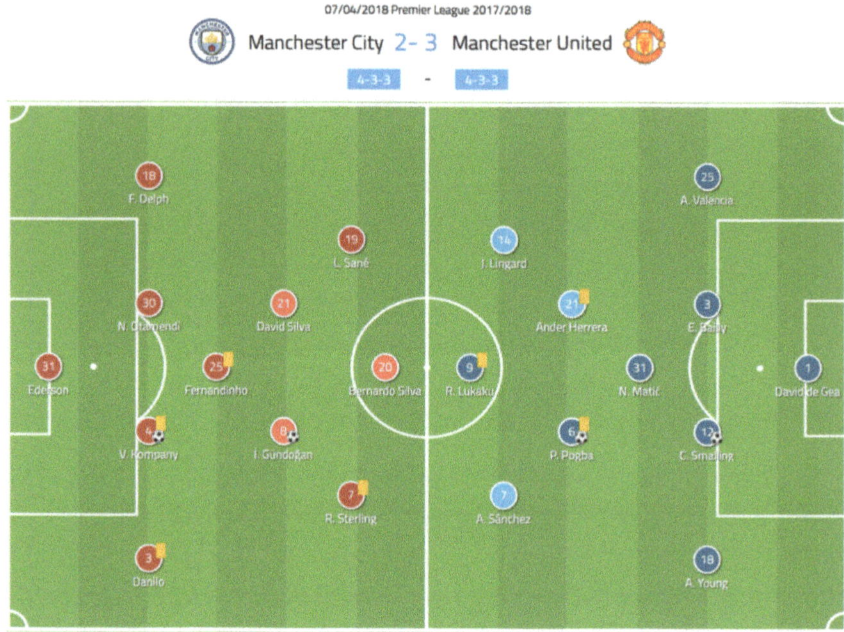

Analyzing the situation

The play starts with the right wing, Bernardo Silva (20), playing to the supporting fullback on the same wing. The fullback passes to defensive midfielder Fernandinho (25), who receives with his far foot with an oriented control. The center forward Sterling (7), comes to support, attracting the center midfielder Matic.

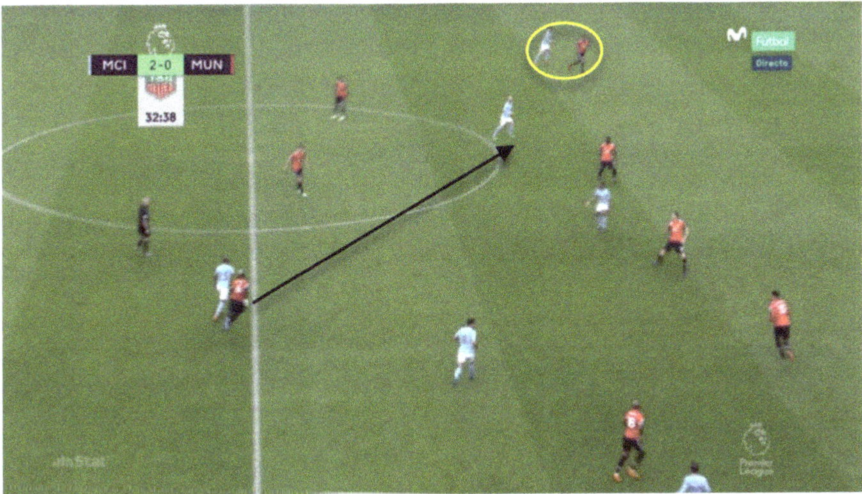

The space in midfield is left with no opposition to cut off the passing line. In three touches, Fernandinho plays quickly to David Silva. It's important that Sané maintains his width to pin the fullback, generating more space between the centerback and the fullback.

Silva controls the ball and is pressed by the right centerback, while

Sterling sees the gap and shows for a pass in the space that has been generated. Sané maintains the width.

ORIENTED CONTROL

Consists of receiving the ball in a way that allows us to execute the next action as quickly and efficiently as possible, whether it's a pass, shot, or dribble. Always controlling with the far foot so that the ball can be controlled comfortably and played quickly. This technical action allows the player to gain time to carry out the next action.

Situation 4: different channels. Overlapping fullback

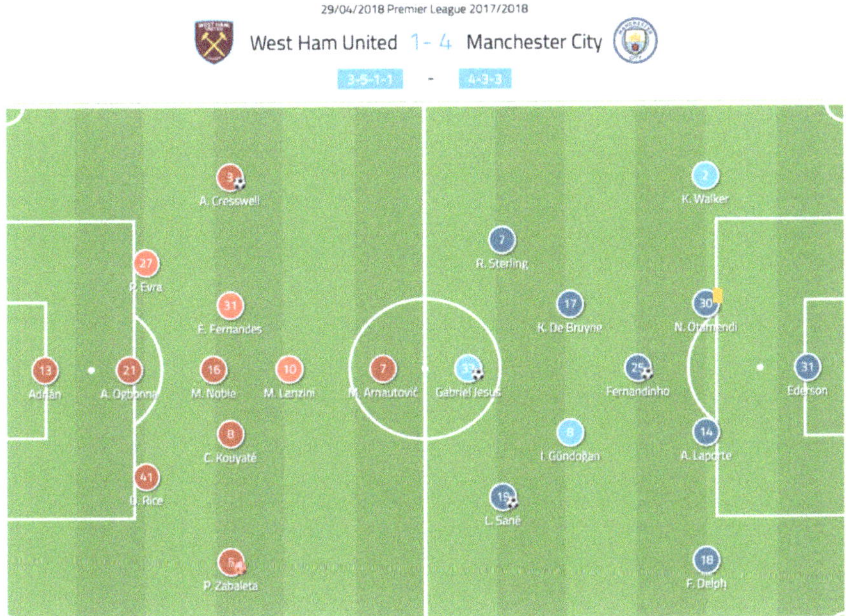

Analyzing the situation

Manchester City starts the play in possession of the ball, with time and space. When the left fullback (18) receives the pass, he begins his advance into the opponent's half of the field with the ball under control.

City's left winger (7) remains positioned inside, not going towards the side of the field, so as not to occupy the same channel as the fullback (18) who is carrying the ball. This produces a triangle between the fullback (18), the winger (7), and the central midfielder (8). Play is switched to the opposite side.

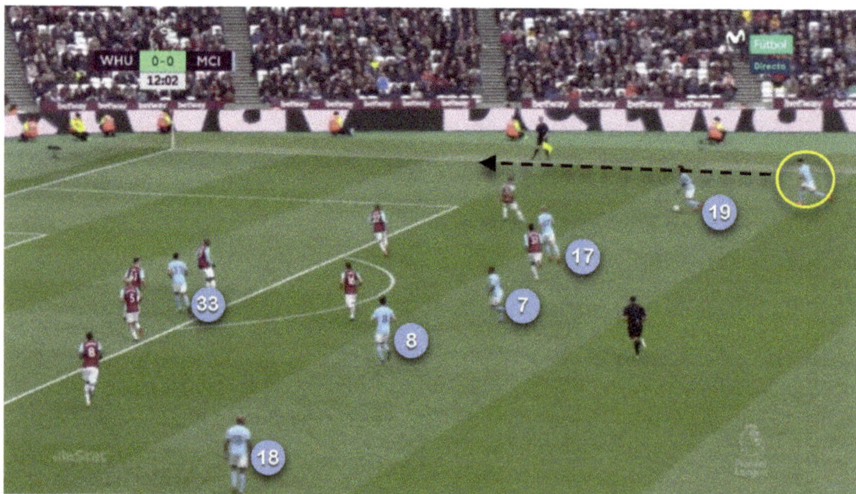

The right winger (19) is now in possession of the ball. He receives the ball and see that the right fullback is overtaking him from behind. This overlapping movement is key, because it creates a distraction and draws the opponent's marking. By overtaking the winger from behind, the fullback gives the player in possession more time to decide his next action, which in this case is to shoot on goal and score.

OVERLAPPING ON THE OUTSIDE

This overtaking movement on the outside of the team mate who has the ball generates two situations..
If the opponent comes out to pressure the ball he will face a 2 v 1.
On the other hand, if the opponent maintains his position and does not come out, it gives more space and time for the player on the ball to make decisions.

Situation 5: offensive disorganization

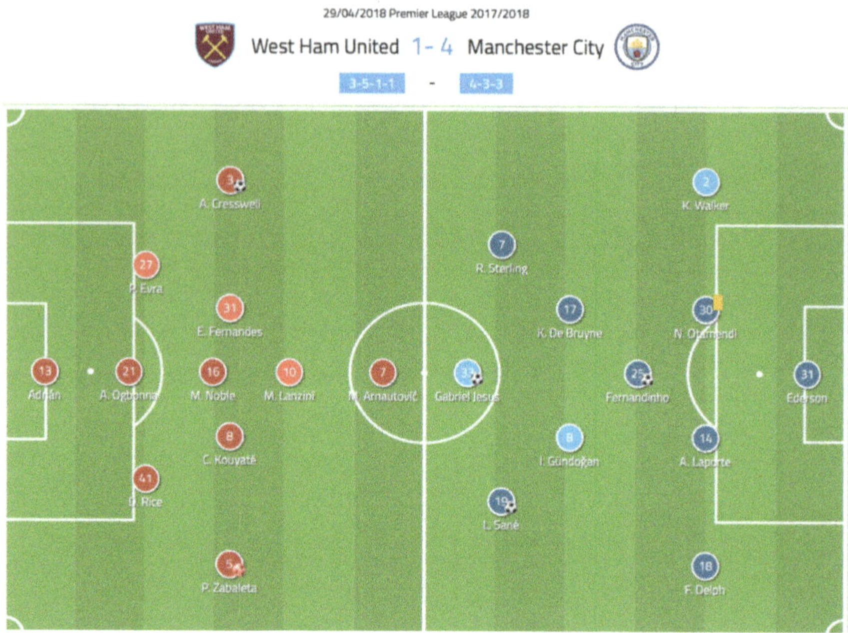

Analyzing the situation

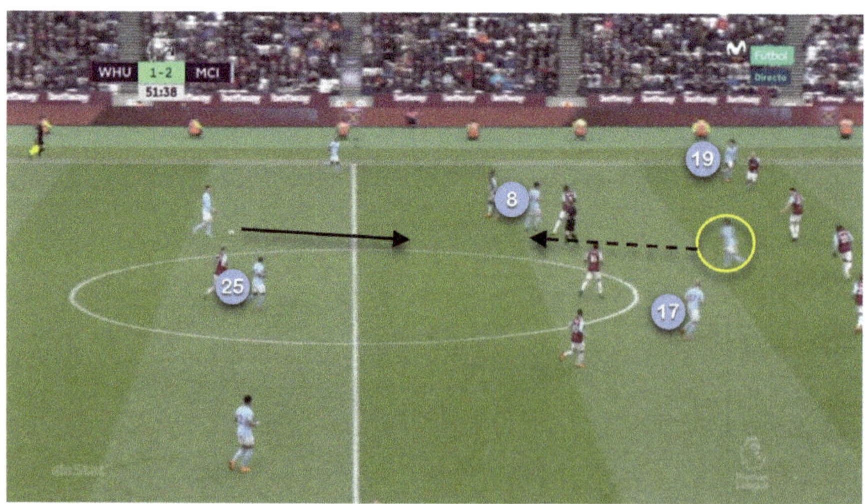

The center defender of Manchester City arrives at the midfield line with the ball under control. The center forward, Gabriel Jesús, drops down to provide a passing option and be closer to the ball in order to help develop the attack.

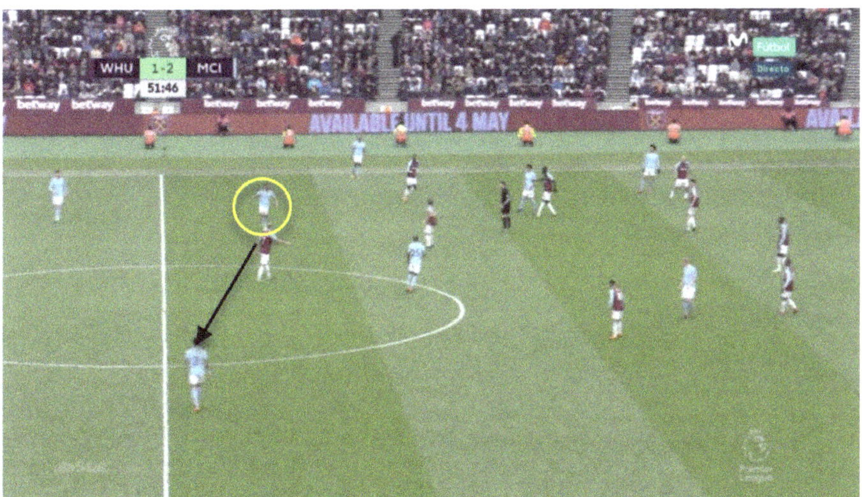

Now in possession Jesús turns to face forward, making himself the focal point of the attack, moving the ball, and being active in order to generate a superiority. This produces offensive disorganization.

Remaining active in the generation of the attack, Jesús sees the dismarking of the right wing (7) at the correct moment and a pass into depth.

After giving this pass to Sterling (7), Jesús continues his run in the direction of the opposing goal. Despite being far away, the Brazilian's objective is to arrive as a passing option inside the penalty area.

Sterling choose to take a little more time and then plays the ball to Gabriel Jesús, who receives and scores.

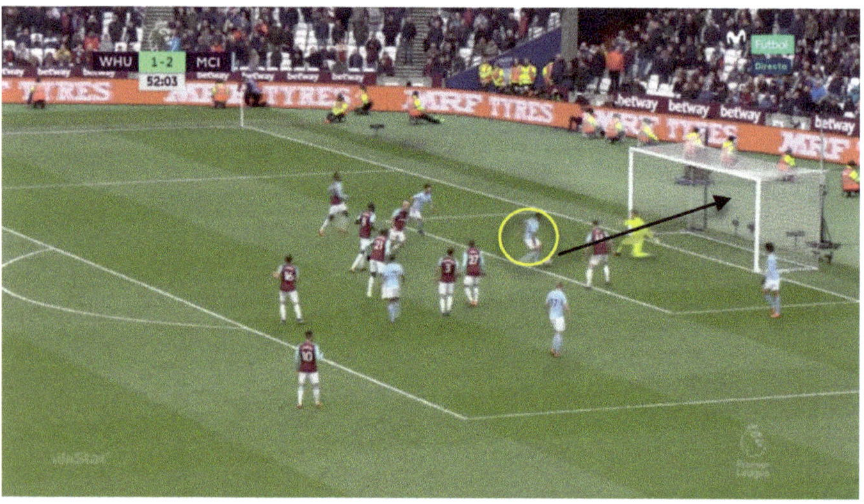

OFFENSIVE DISORDER

When the opponent is organized defensively in their own half of the field and their lines are very close together, it makes the team compact. If our team can't move or "disorder" them (for example, when the center forward drops), we won't generate space, and the opponent will identify their marking references very easily.

ALWAYS ARRIVE

It's better to arrive in the penalty area than to wait there. If you are waiting in the area, then the opponent will be on top of you, as opposed to arriving and surprising the defender, who can lose sight of his mark.

CHAPTER 2

SARRI

INTRODUCTION

Usual system of play. Used in 97% of the games.

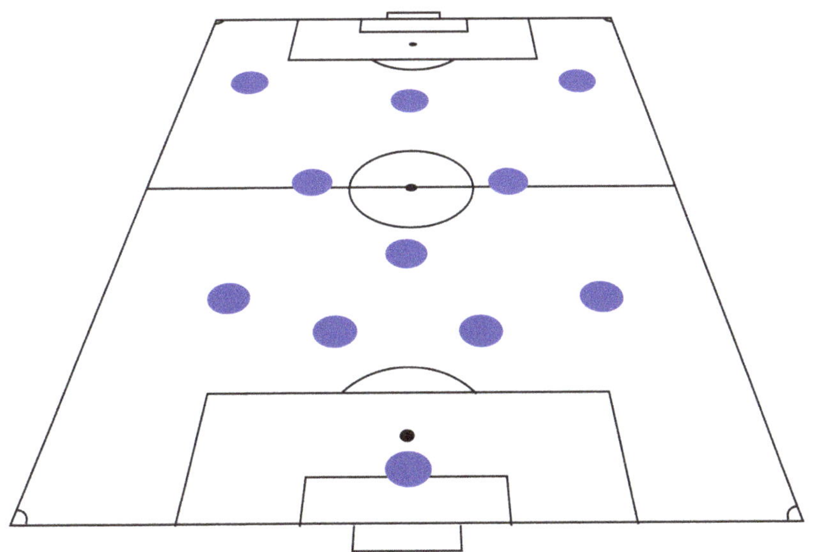

1-4-3-3

Keys to Sarri's organized attack

- Prioritize arriving in midfield with the ball under control
- Superiorities
- Rapid circulation of the ball
- Use of the third man
- Dismarking
- Attacking fullbacks
- Wingers creating offensive disorganization

BUILDOUT THROUGH THE GOAL KICK

Situation 1: buildout through the centerback - under pressure - progression through the opposite side

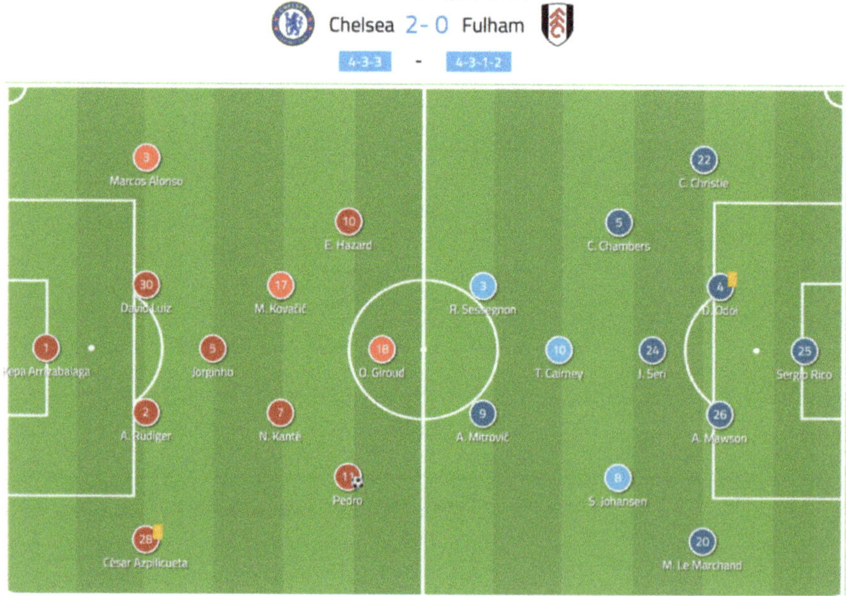

Analyzing the situation

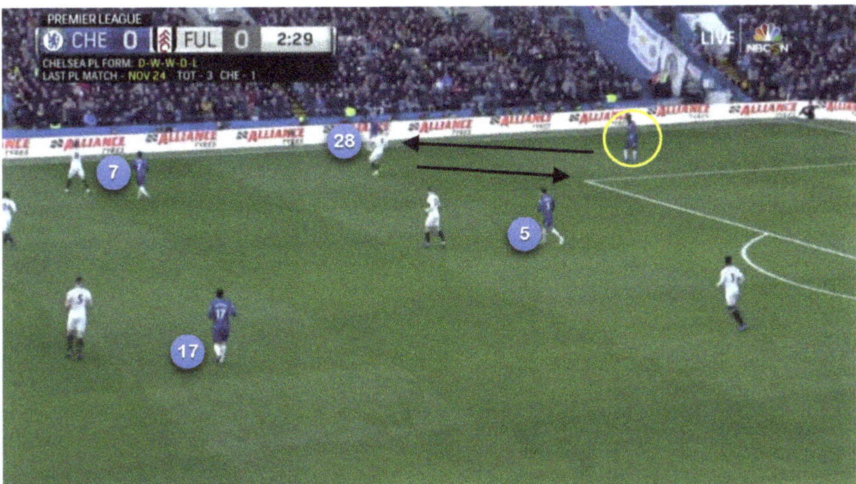

The goalkeeper, Kepa Arrizabalaga, takes the goal kick quickly, playing short to the right centerback Antonio Rüdiger. Rüdiger controls and plays to the right fullback César Azpilicueta (28), who is closed down by one of the opposing forwards. Because the right midfielder N'Golo Kanté (7) finds himself marked by the left center midfielder of Fulham, and the defensive midfielder Jorginho (5) is marked by the attacking midfielder, there is no clear passing option, and for this reason he turns to play back to the centerback.

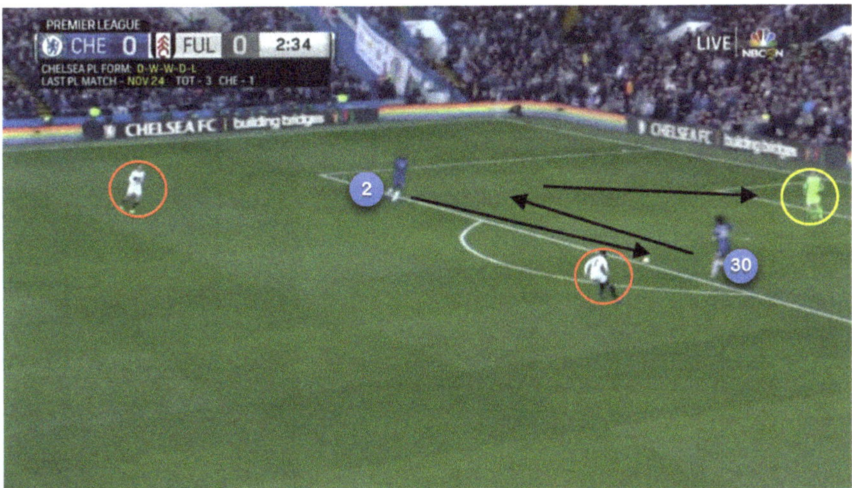

David Luiz (30), the left centerback, draws near to Rüdiger (2) to offer a passing alternative. This produces a 3 v 2 against the two opposing forwards, with the goalkeeper providing the numerical superiority. Once Luiz returns the pass to Rüdiger he continues to run a few meters towards the midfield, dragging the forward who is marking him and generating more time and space for the goalkeeper, Arrizabalaga, who can now play out through the fullback on the opposite side from where the buildout was started.

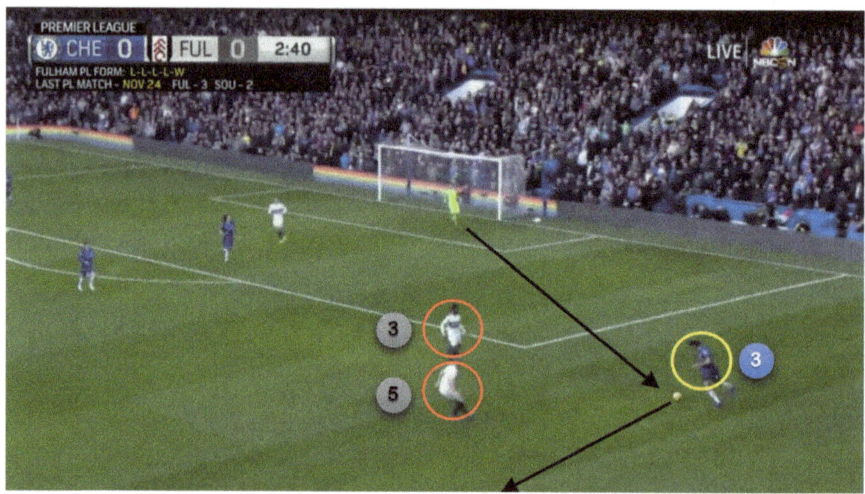

Marcos Alonso drops down from the left wing to be a passing option, receives the ball, and is pressured by the forward (3) who was marking David Luiz and by the right center midfielder (5). In this way, two opposing players have been attracted. When the opponent's right center midfielder moves up to pressure, it frees up his marking reference, who is the left center midfielder Mateo Kovačić (17).

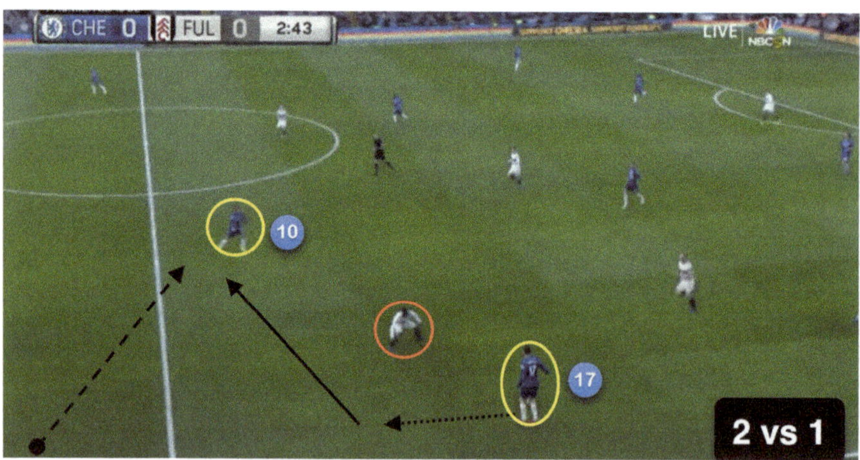

Kovačić (17) goes to the wing to be a passing option for the fullback Marcos Alonso. If Kovačić had maintained his position, he would have been marked by the defensive midfielder of Fulham. This movement to the outside causes doubts for the opponent. Does he stay with him and leave the central zone open? Or does he stay in his position and leave the opponent free to receive the ball all alone? He decides to press and stays in the middle of the field, and the left winger Eden Hazard (10) sees the space being created and dismarks towards the center of the field, provoking a 2v1.

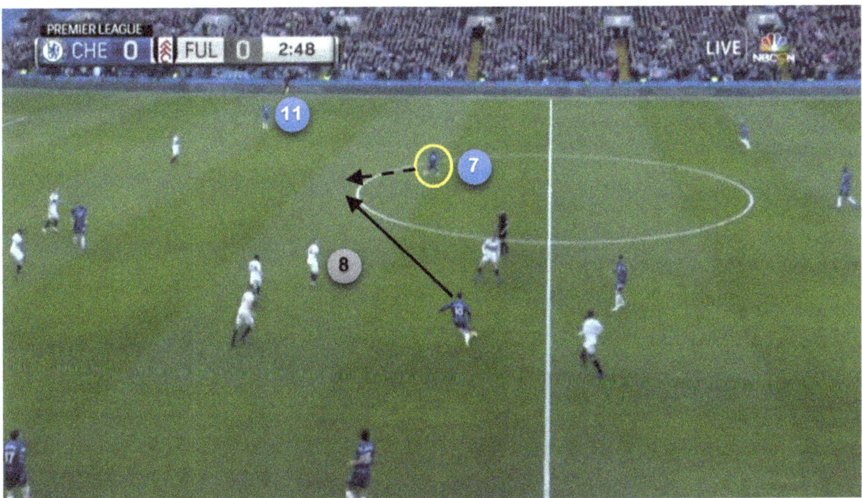

When Hazard receives the ball, he manages to turn and face forward. No longer able to mark his immediate opponent, (8) drops back diagonally. This leaves Kanté, in his position and the right center midfielder, open to receive the ball. Hazard passes to Kanté, who runs with the ball until he unloads it to Pedro, the right winger, who finds himself in width and finishes the attack with a low cross.

THE GOALKEEPER, KEY TO PLAYING OUT

If we want to achieve a clean and effective buildout when faced with good positioning and high pressure from our opponent, it's key that we use our goalkeeper because this player allows us to achieve a numerical superiority in the starting zone. In this way, we're able to have one more option available. It is very important to give the goalkeeper passing options so that he can resolve situations rapidly when the opponent continues to pressure.

Situation 2: buildout through the centerback - under pressure - progression through the same sector.

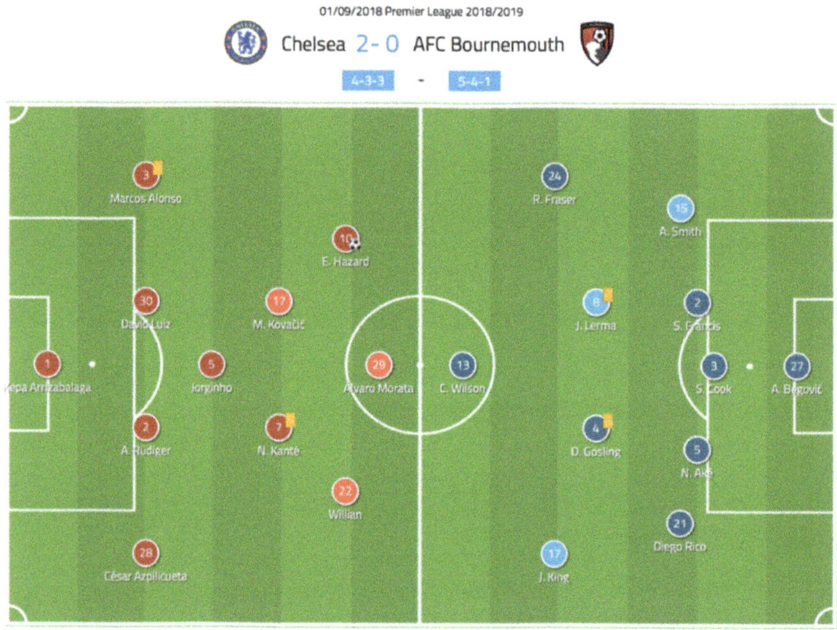

Analyzing the situation

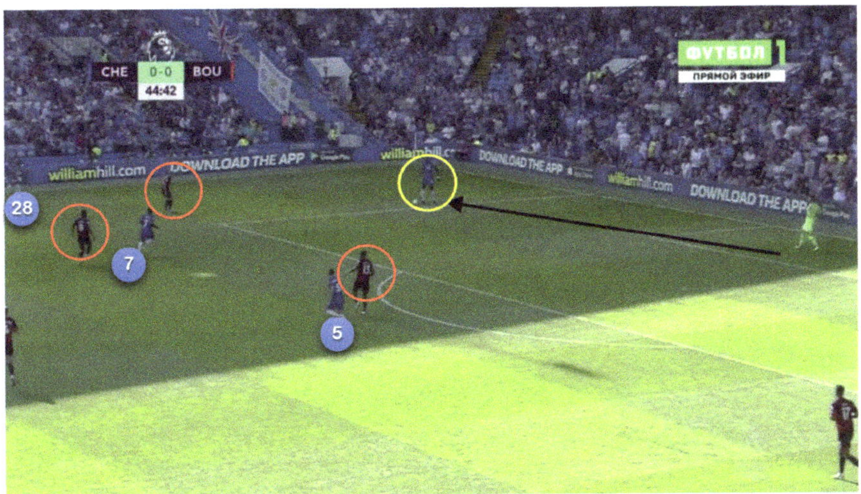

The goalkeeper Arrizabalaga puts the goal kick rapidly into play to Rüdiger (2), the right centerback. There are three passing options going forward, but all of them are marked: Azpilicueta (right fullback, 28), Kanté (right midfielder, 7), and Jorginho (defensive midfielder, 5).

Willian (22) appears as a fourth option for Rüdiger (2) by coming near and offering himself as a passing option in front of his marker.

Rüdiger plays a hard pass to Willian. Kanté (7) interprets the situation, understands that he has an opponent on him, and goes to offer Willian

support. The idea of the third man appears here very clearly.

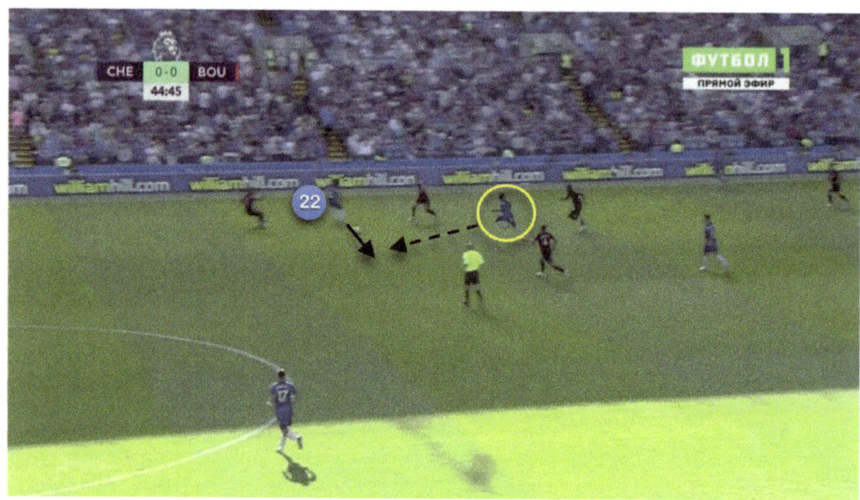

Willian first plays with Kanté, who controls and accelerates, leaving 6 opponents out of the play and behind the line of the ball.

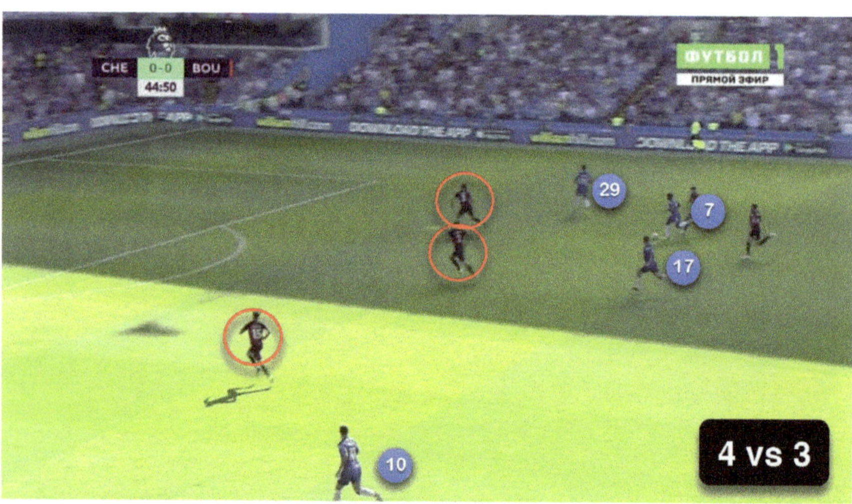

This generates a situation of 4v3 numerical superiority in the attack; made up of Willian, the center forward (29), the left midfielder (17), and the left winger (10).

PASSING OPTIONS FOR THOSE WITH THE BALL AND FOR THOSE WHO WILL RECEIVE IT

In order to build out under the pressure of an opponent in equal numbers, we have to look for a pass that will overcome the opponent's first line of pressure. This can be achieved through a dismarking support by a player who is farther away and is positioned in front of his maker and a third player who comes to support. This last player, with just a change of pace towards the receiver of the pass, can leave his marker behind.

Situation 3: buildout through the fullback – high positioning from the opponent

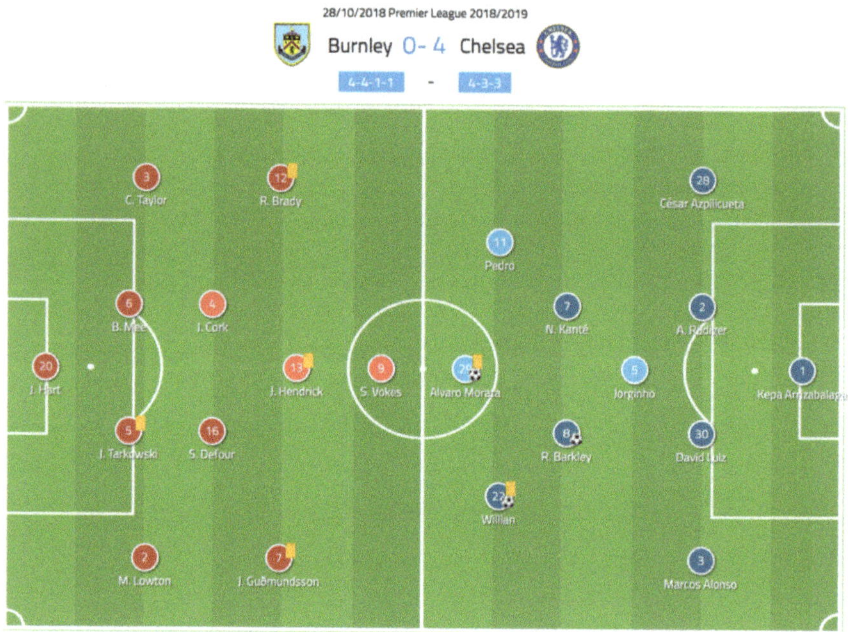

Analyzing the situation

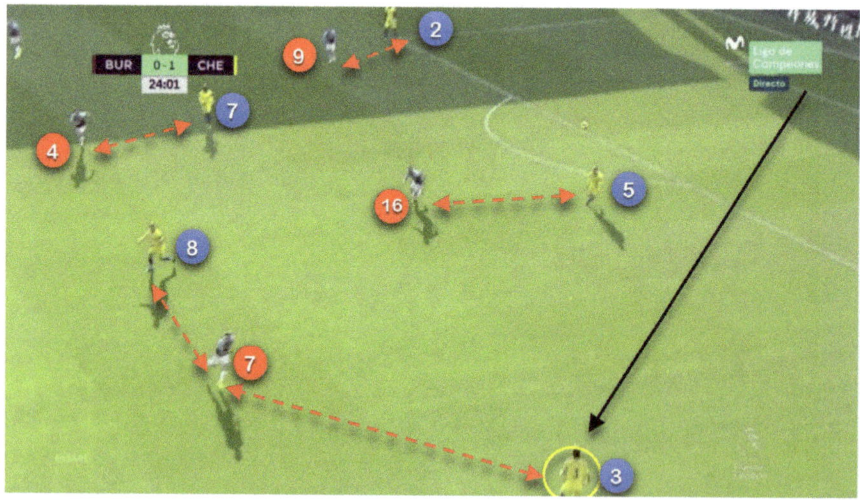

Burnley opts to position themselves high in order to prevent Chelsea from building out comfortably. They also decide to use their two centerbacks to keep center forward Alvaro Morata occupied (2v1), which means they have one less player in the opposing half of the field. So Chelsea finds a 2v1: fullback-center midfielder vs center midfielder. The goalkeeper Kepa Arrizablalaga plays to the left fullback Marcos Alonso (3).

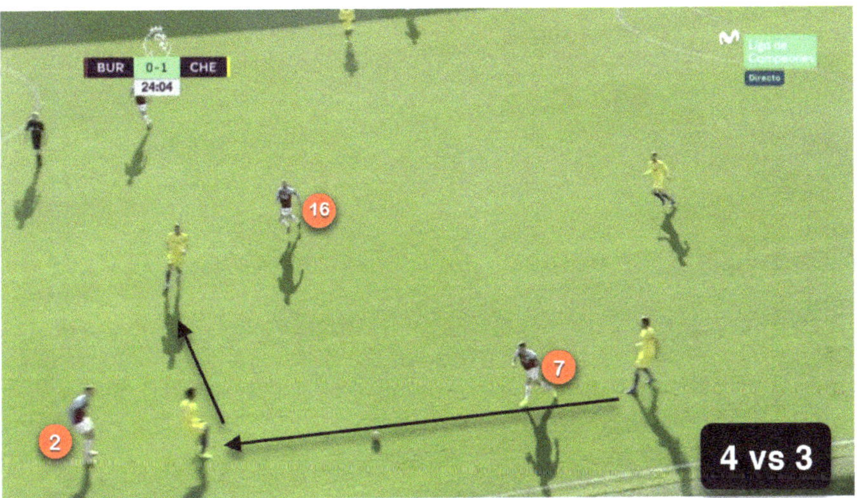

Alonso (3) controls the ball and is pressed by the right winger (7), while Willian (22) shows as an option in front of the right fullback (2) to create a numerical superiority in this section of the field. Alonso (3) plays to Willian (22), who plays first time to Ross Barkley (8), the right center midfielder. At the same time, defensive midfielder Jorginho (5) offers support.

Jorginho (5) has become the free man because his marking reference has gone to pressure Barkley (8). Despite the opponent's attempt to prevent them from building out comfortably, Chelsea's clean buildout allows them to organize their attack.

PROGRESSION - FINISHING

Situation 1: winger between the lines

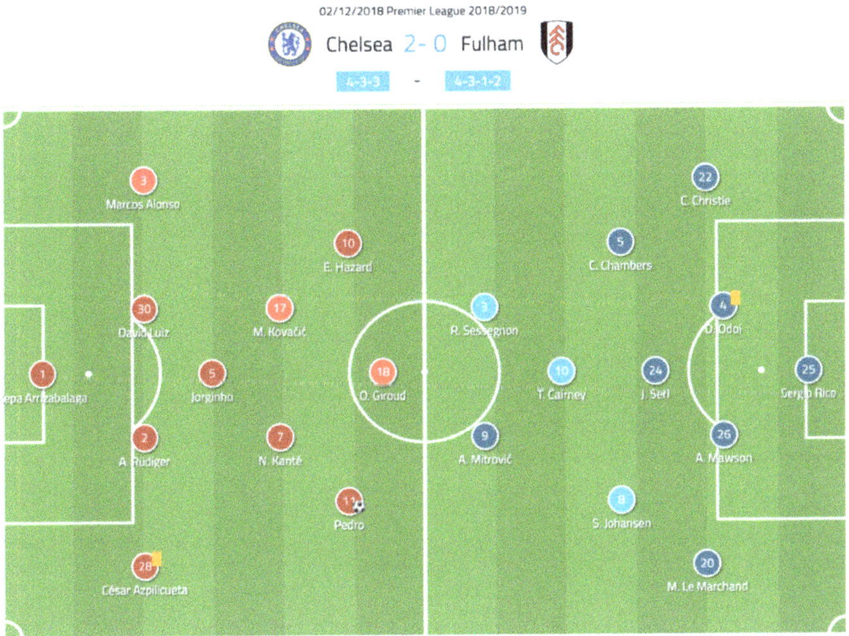

Analyzing the situation

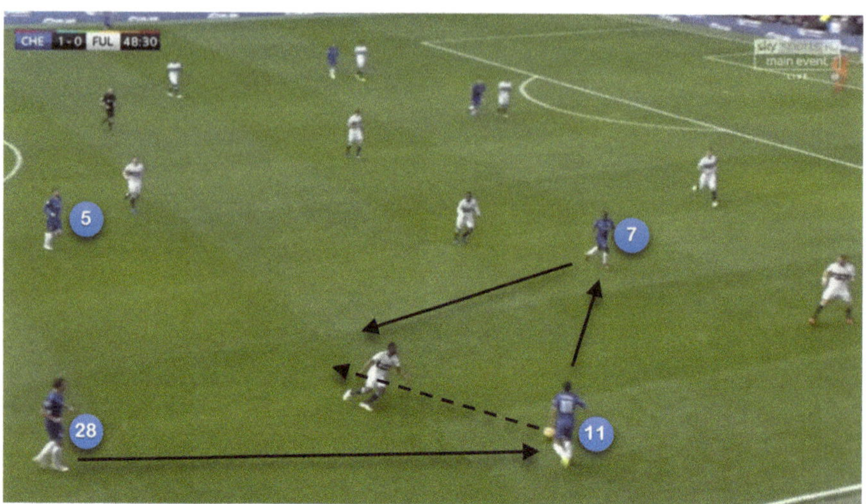

Fulham starts the second half by changing their system to a 4-4-1-1. Azpilicueta (28, right fullback), plays to Pedro (11, right winger) who is dropping down, while Kanté (7, right center midfielder) advances to provide depth. Pedro does a wall pass with Kanté, taking a touch, passing, and receiving the ball again. Then, because he finds no space to progress, Pedro plays to Jorginho (5 defensive midfielder), who is offering support.

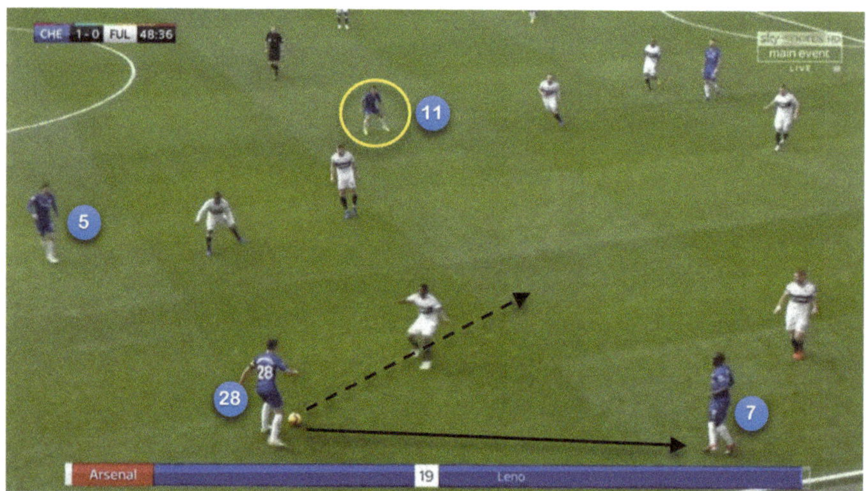

Jorginho (5) turns to play to Azpilicueta (28), who finds himself under pressure from the opponent. For this reason Kanté (7) drops back to show himself as an option, and the concept of give and go appears again.

Azpilicueta passes to Kanté and then moves forward without the ball, leaving the zone in order to free up space for Kanté.

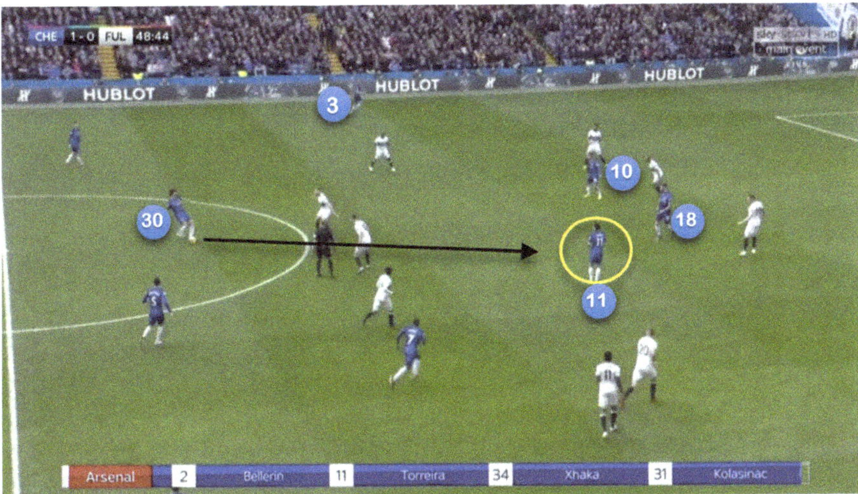

Kanté runs forward with the ball and plays to the second centerback (30) since the first centerback (2) is being marked by one of the forwards (9). David Luiz (30) advances with the ball and launches a pass between the lines towards Pedro (11), who has remained in this area of the field. Chelsea's left fullback (3) maintains the width and the winger, Hazard (10), is positioned inside, near the centerbacks, creating a 2v2 with the center forward Olivier Giroud (18). These actions make it so that Pedro can receive the ball and turn, because the centerbacks can't leave the line to pressure the ball without leaving Hazard or Giroud free.

The winger and the forward start to run forward, looking to dismark and forcing the defenders to retreat with them. In this way, it gives Pedro the time and space to advance, prepare his body, and shoot.

PASS AND MOVE

The action of passing and moving has two consequences: 1) It eliminates the opponent who comes to pressure the player who executes the first pass.
2) It creates more time/space for the player who receives the ball first. This time and space is created if the opponent allows himself to be dragged away by following the player who started the wall pass.

Situation 2: generating space on the wing to create depth

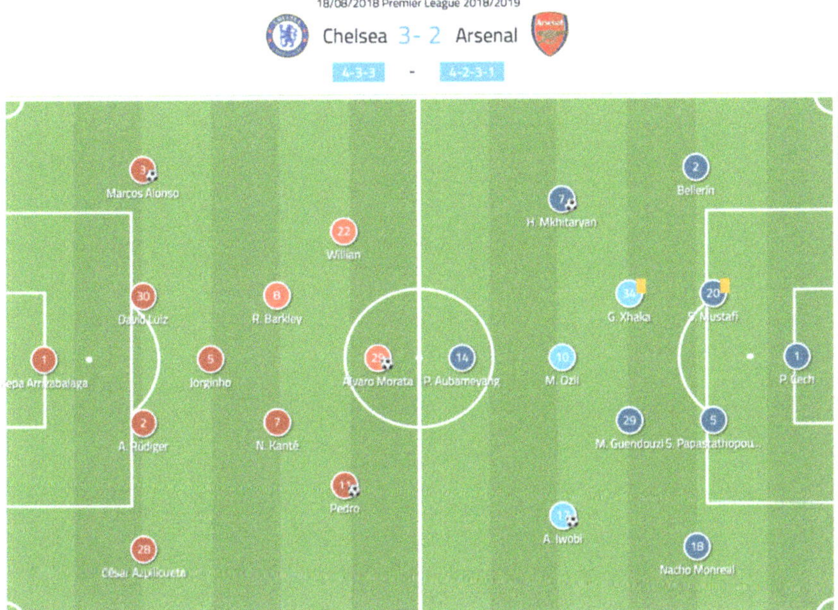

Analyzing the situation

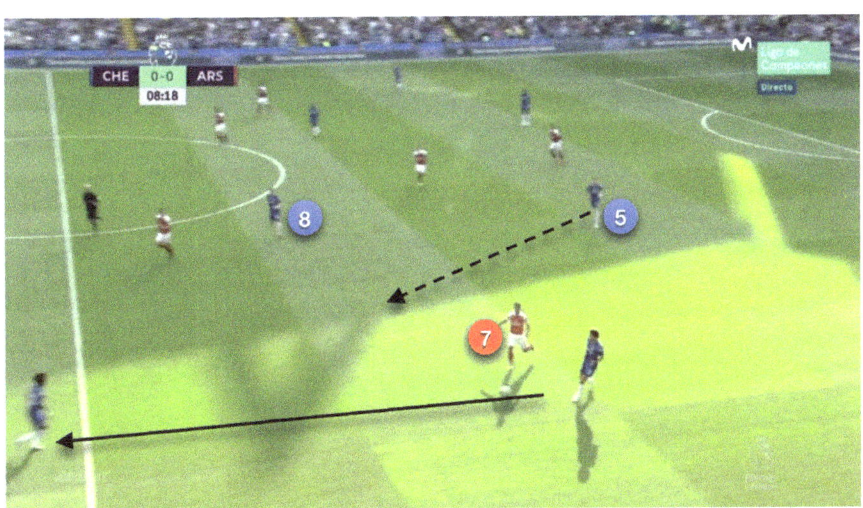

David Luiz (30) plays to Alonso (3), who is pressured by the opponent's right winger (7), which is the reason Willian (22) decides to drop back. Jorginho (5), the defensive midfielder, moves up quickly to give Willian support.

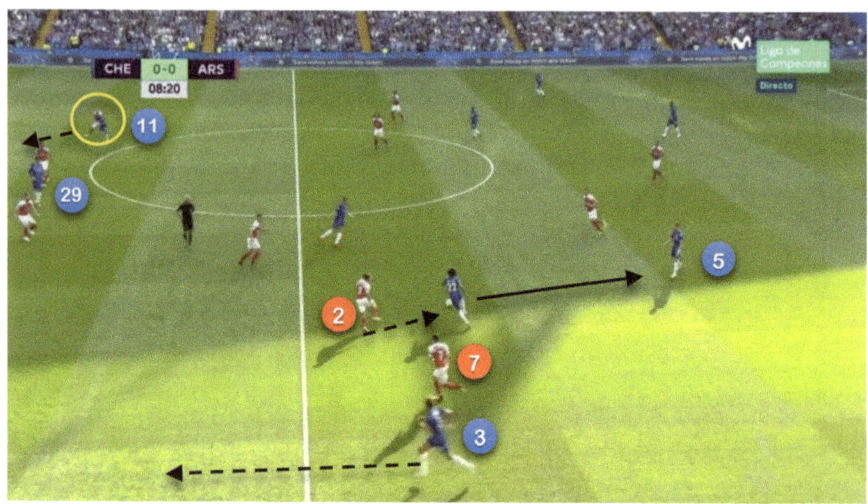

Willian (22) controls the ball and comes inside. In order to become an option, Pedro (11) dismarks into depth in front of the left fullback, knowing that the defensive line is in a high position. The opposing left fullback (2) decides to leave the line to pressure Willian (22), which generates a free space in this section of the field that Alonso (3) takes advantage of. Willian (22) plays to the supporting Jorginho (5) and this player plays a long pass into space for Alonso to run onto. It's very important that the center forward, Morata (29), continues to pin the centerbacks.

Alonso touches the ball forward, on a diagonal towards the goal. Pedro (11), who has already dismarked in order to become an option for Willian (22), uses this action to remain in the central attacking zone. This is why it's Pedro who receives the assist from Alonso and scores for Chelsea.

Situation 3: the fullback's surprise

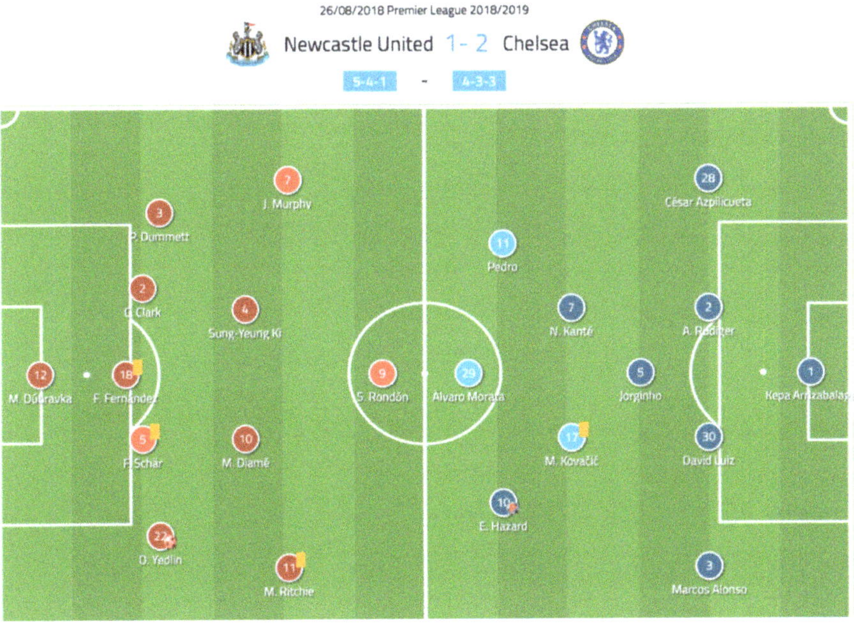

Analyzing the situation

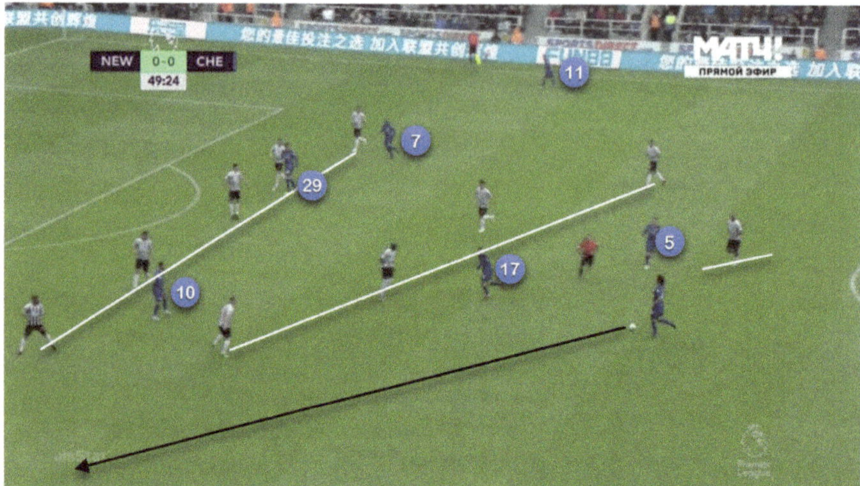

Newcastle is organized defensively in a low block. Chelsea is circulating the ball. David Luiz (30) is running with the ball and decides to play forward to Alonso (3). We can see that Kanté (7) finds himself on top of the last line. Hazard (10) is positioned inside, and Pedro (11) maintains the width.

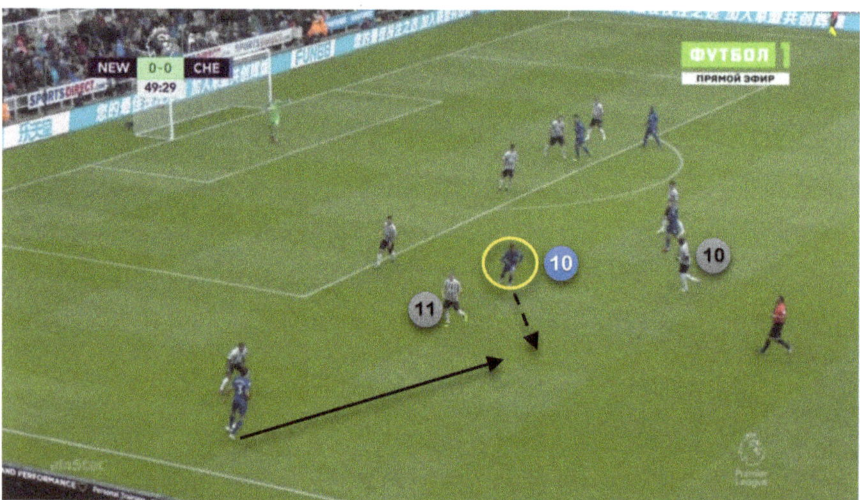

Alonso (3) receives the ball and faces pressure from the opponent, so he decides to turn and play back to Hazard, who is dropping down to show himself as an option. In his route to Newcastle's midfield line, Hazard (10) appears between the right winger (11), dropping down behind his back, and the right center midfielder (10).

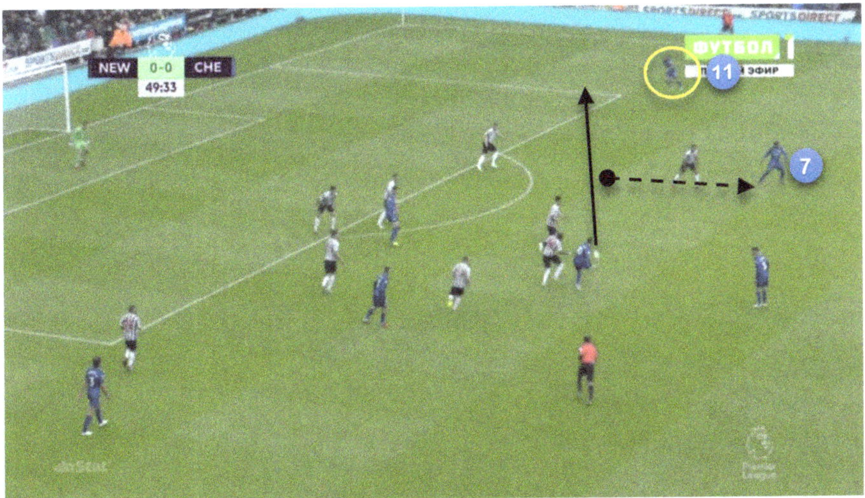

Kanté (7) who was pinning the left fullback (3), drops back to return his position. Pedro (11) who was wide at the start of this progression, receives the ball from Hazard (10).

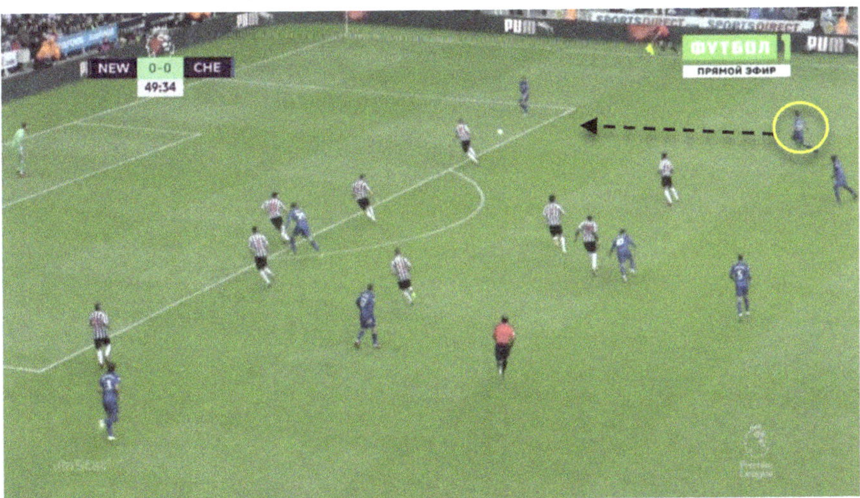

Azpilaceuta (28), sensing the possibility of getting involved, appears on the scene, changes the pace of his run, offers a support to Pedro, and finishes the move with a shot inside the area.

This attacking and finishing situation, which results in a shot inside the area by the fullback, can occur when the opponent has become extremely compact and is rigidly marking with a high density of players.

Situation 4: running with the ball – it's not always passing

Analyzing the situation

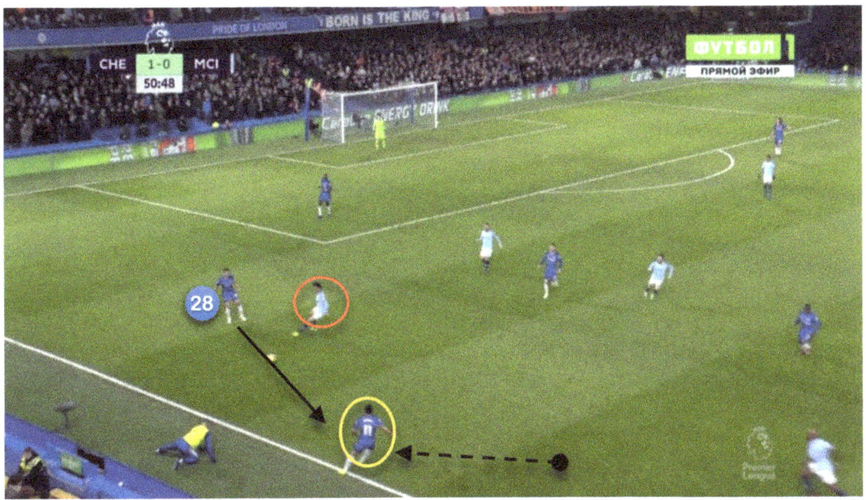

After good ball circulation by Chelsea in the starting zone, Manchester City decides to initiate the press when the ball arrives to the right fullback, Azpilicueta (28). While being pressed by the left wing, Sané (19), Azpilicueta sees a passing option in Pedro (11), who acts quickly to drop down diagonally towards the ball, moving behind the pressure of Sané.

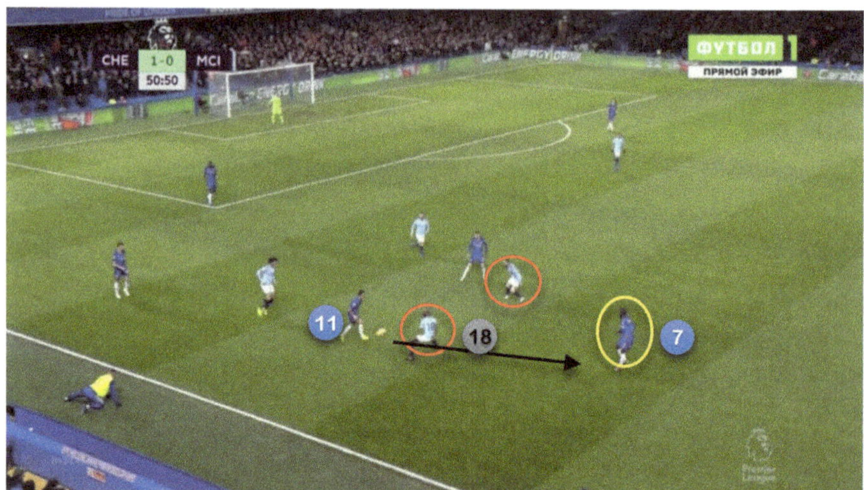

Pedro (11) has time to turn, and is pressured by Delph (18). Kanté (7) sees the space generated by the pressure of City's left fullback (18) and receives the ball alone and unmarked because the opposing center midfielder (25) has decided not to pressure him.

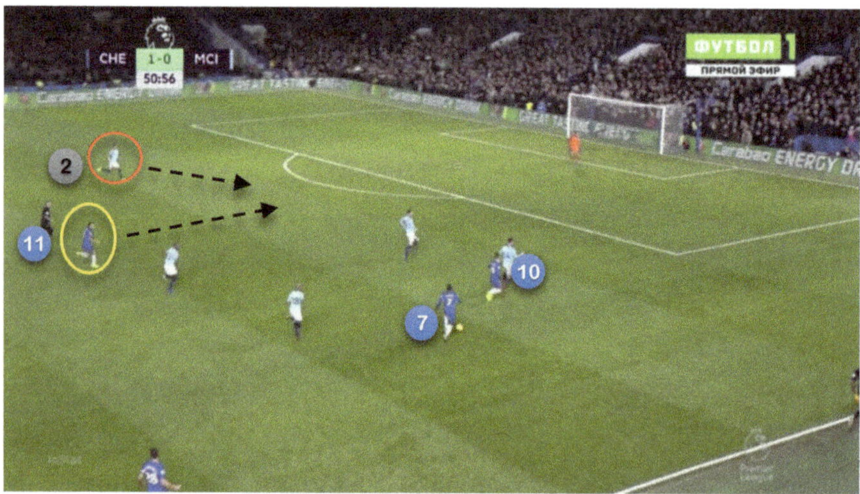

Kanté (7), with time and space, runs with the ball. He changes his rhythm and leaves seven opposing players behind. He has Hazard dismarking (10) and Pedro (11), who started the play, is also an option. Pedro's run through the middle forces City's right back (2) to attempt to close him down. Kanté (7), still not being pressured, continues to run with the ball.

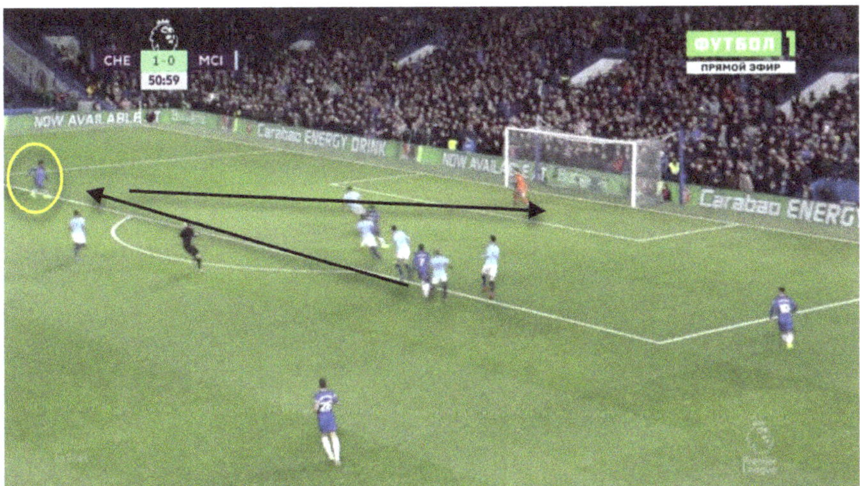

Walker (2) closes down, which frees up Chelsea's left winger Willian (22), who is now unmarked. Kanté (7) passes the ball at the right moment. The fact that Kanté is able to take more time to read the situation allows his pass to find Willian in a great position to convert the scoring chance.

Situation 5: interior play

Analyzing the situation

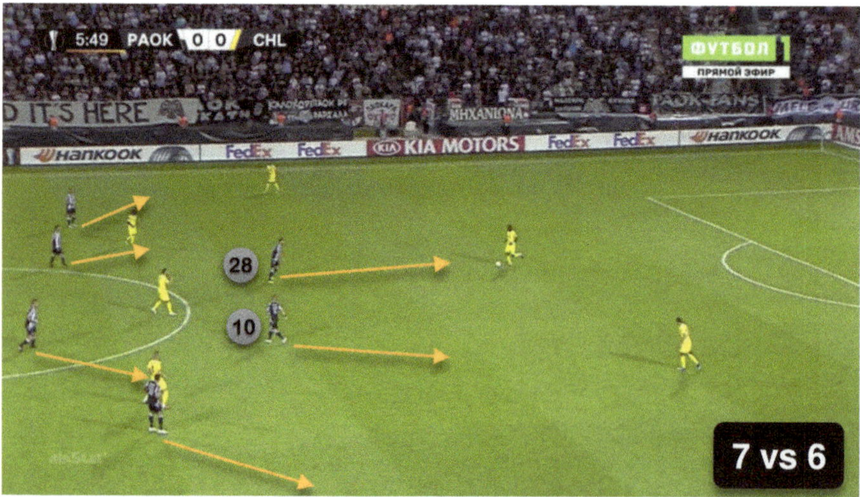

PAOK takes up an intermediate position. Their four midfielders, the attacking midfielder (28), and the center forward (10) are all waiting for Chelsea's attack. The centerback Rüdiger (2) has time to advance. Evaluating the marking references, he observes that Chelsea has a 7 vs 6 numerical superiority, which includes the left fullback (3) who does not appear in this image.

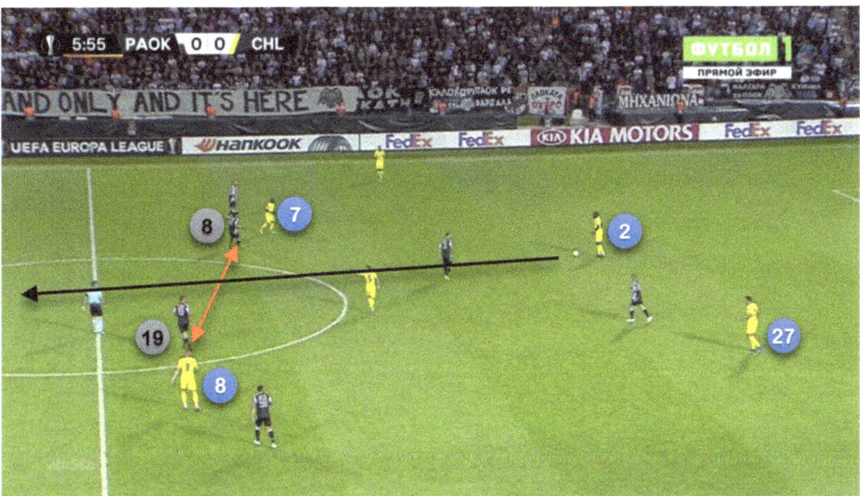

The centerbacks (2 and 27) pass the ball in order to make the opponent move. In this sequence of passes, space is generated between the two opposing center midfielders because their marking references are the center midfielders Kanté (7) and Barkley (8).

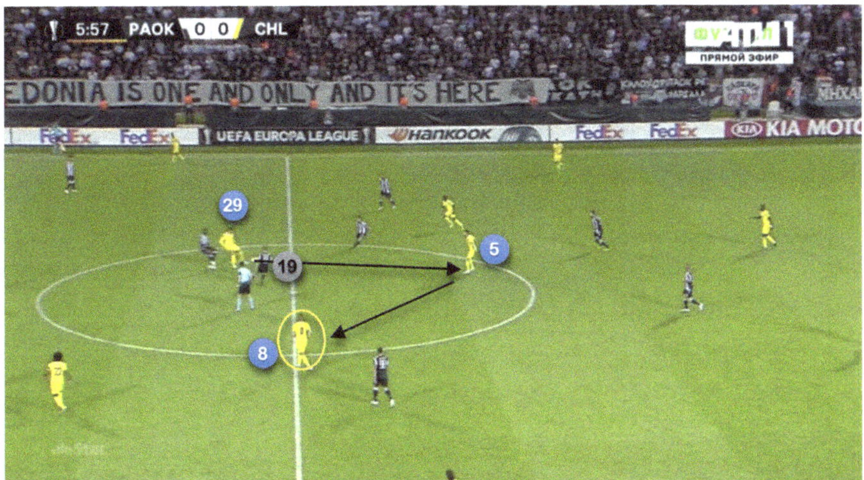

The center Forward Morata (29) drops down into the midfield in order to become an option. Upon receiving the pass from the right centerback (2), the right center midfielder (19) comes to pressure him, which leaves Barkley (8) free. Morata plays to the defensive midfielder Jorginho (5), who is showing to support in the direction Morata is facing, and breaks lines with a quick pass to the unmarked Barkley.

Barkley (8) controls the ball and is pressured by the right fullback (20) which leaves Willian (22) unmarked, because Willian was this player's marking reference. Barkley overcomes his opponent and runs with the ball towards the right centerback (34), who he pins and then plays a pass to Willian at the perfect moment. Goal for Chelsea.

WHO IS PRESSURING ME? WHO IS LEAVING ME FREE?

According to the system they face, every player will have an initial marking reference. We will see this change in the game, due to the circulation of the ball and the movement of the players. When a player in possession of the ball is pressured, and he is not that opponent's initial reference, this will free up a teammate to become unmarked. This will happen whenever the changes in marking aren't a previously coordinated defensive scheme designed to prevent the situation.

libro
futbol
.com
AL GOL SE
LLEGA LEYENDO

CHAPTER 3

POCHETTINO

INTRODUCTION

USUAL SYSTEM OF PLAY. USED IN 40% OF THE GAMES

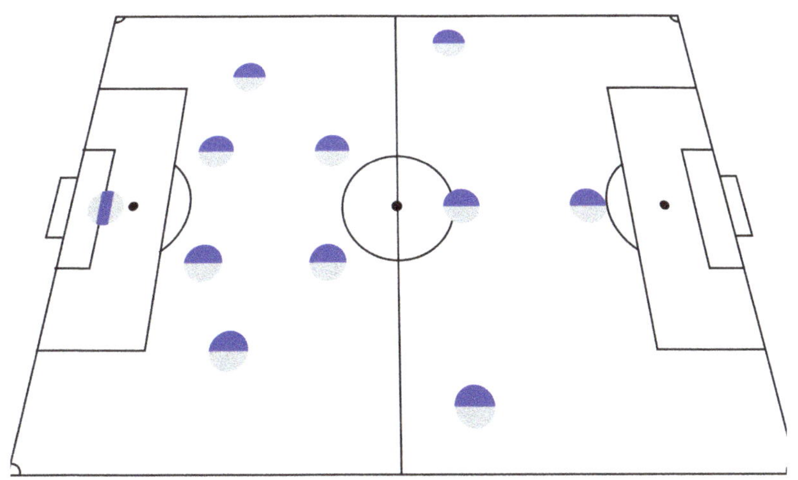

1-4-2-3-1

KEY POINTS TO POCHETTINO'S ORGANIZED ATTACK

- Prioritize arriving in the middle of the field with the ball under control
- Rapid circulation of the ball
- Use of the third man
- Occupation of space
- Attacking fullbacks
- Offensive disorganization through the wingers
- Dropping down/moving up

BUILDING OUT THROUGH THE GOAL KICK

Situation 1: long buildout - winning the second ball and continuing play

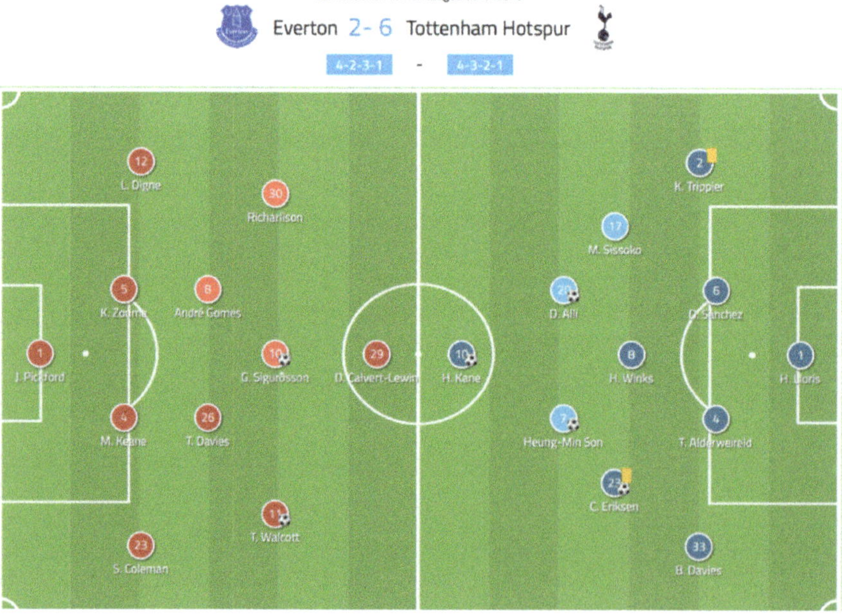

Analyzing the situation

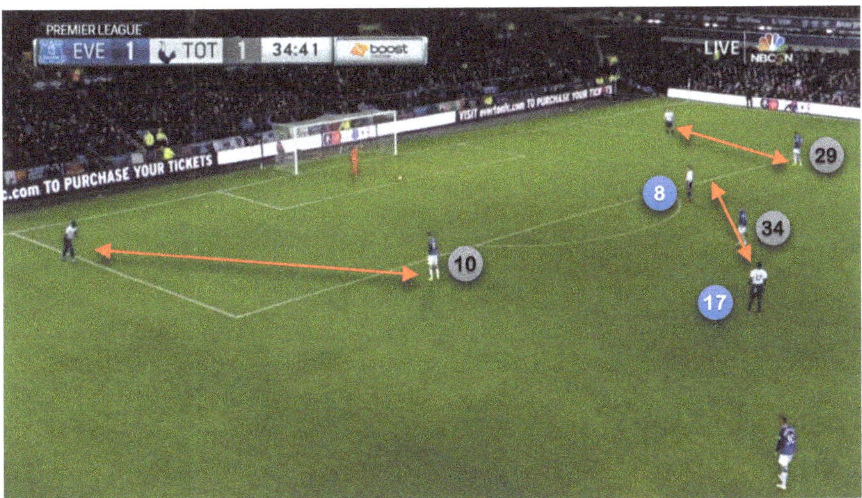

Tottenham sets up for a short passing buildup, with the central defenders open and the defensive midfielder as an option at the top of the penalty area. Everton pushes up their right midfielder (26) to position him in a way that allows him to cover two passing options: to the defensive midfielder (8) and to the right midfielder (17). The center forward (29) and the attacking midfielder (10) watch the centerbacks.

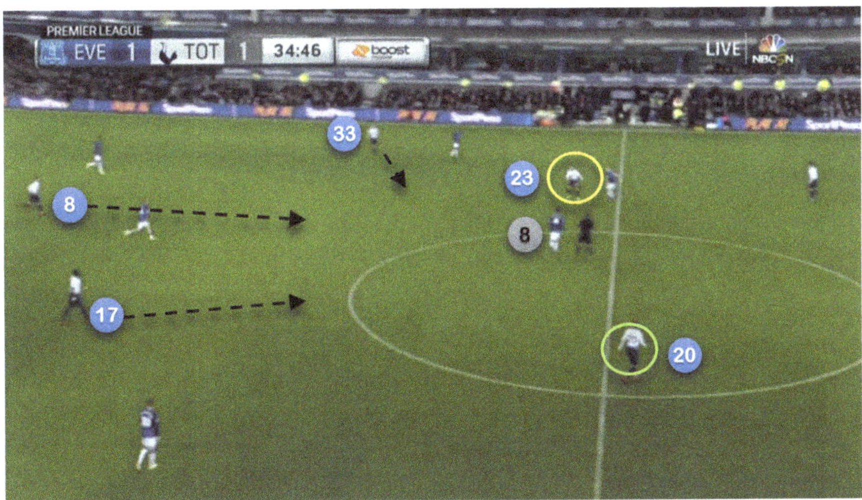

The goalkeeper Lloris plays a long direct pass to the left center midfielder Eriksen (23), who jumps to dispute the ball with the right fullback (23). This produces a rapid reorganization for Tottenham. As many players as

possible converge on the zone where the ball will drop, with the intention of winning the second ball. Everton's left midfielder (8) also comes to the ball, which frees up Spur's right attacking midfielder Deli Alli (20).

The second ball is won by the left fullback Davies (33). He heads the ball to right attacking midfielder Sissoko (17), who plays a wall pass with Dele Alli (20).

Since Everton's right fullback (23) did not recover his position rapidly, the left attacking midfielder Son (7) takes advantage of this empty space. Sissoko (17) finds him quickly and his pass into depth creates a clear goal scoring situation. The center forward Kane (10) decides to maintain his

position in the central attacking zone, pinning the opponent's centerbacks.

WINNING THE SECOND BALL AFTER DISPUTING A LONG GOAL KICK

When the opponent's positioning reduces the possibilities of playing short and the goal kick is played long, it's important that the nearest players close in to a circumference of less than 5 meters from where the ball will drop and be disputed. This will give them the highest probability of winning the second ball.

Situation 2: long pass – Man to man marking situation

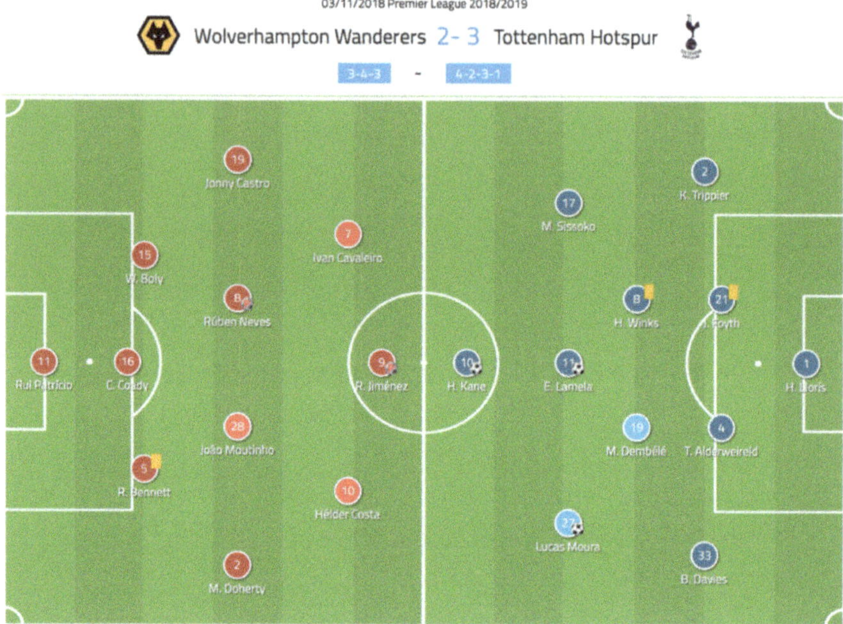

Analyzing the situation

Wolverhampton opts to take up a high position to try and prevent Tottenham from playing out short. Tottenham always open up their centerbacks and have one of their midfielders come near to offer an option to play short.

The opponent marks man to man, setting up a series of individual duels. Faced with this situation, the goalkeeper Lloris decides to play long towards the zone where the center forward Kane (10) and Erik Lamela (11) have created a 2 v 2. The player who jumps with Kane to dispute the aerial ball is not the player who was marking him, but the player who was marking Lamela. Kane wins the aerial duel, knocking the ball down to Lamela's feet.

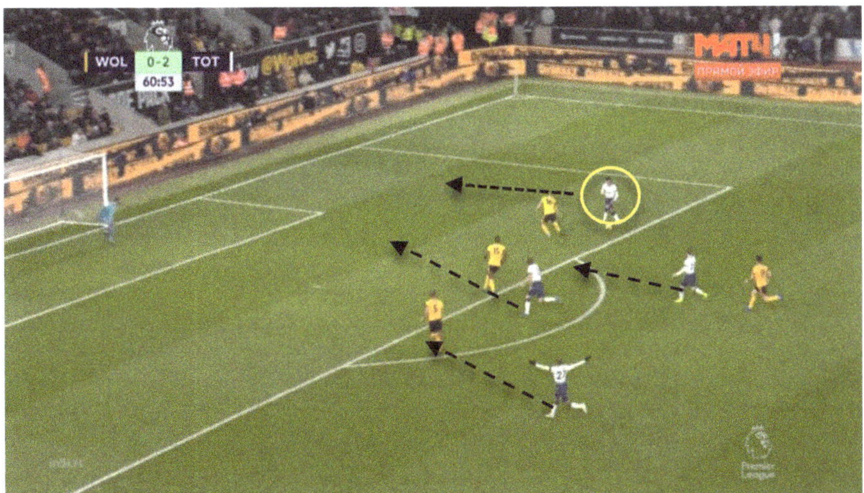

Lamela (11) plays a 1 v 1 duel inside the area, gaining depth and then passing back to Kane (10). The center forward is able to convert the chance after a rebound. A goal scoring situation created with just three touches.

LONG GOAL KICK – MAN TO MAN MARKING SITUATION

If the opponent offers us individual duels on our goal kicks, and we have a player we can count on for his aerial ability, we need to make this player the priority for our long passing options. At the same time, it is necessary to have a team mate, preferably one with excellent 1 v 1 ability, near him to be the primary receiver of the ball.

Situation 3: buildout through the centerback – opponent positioned high

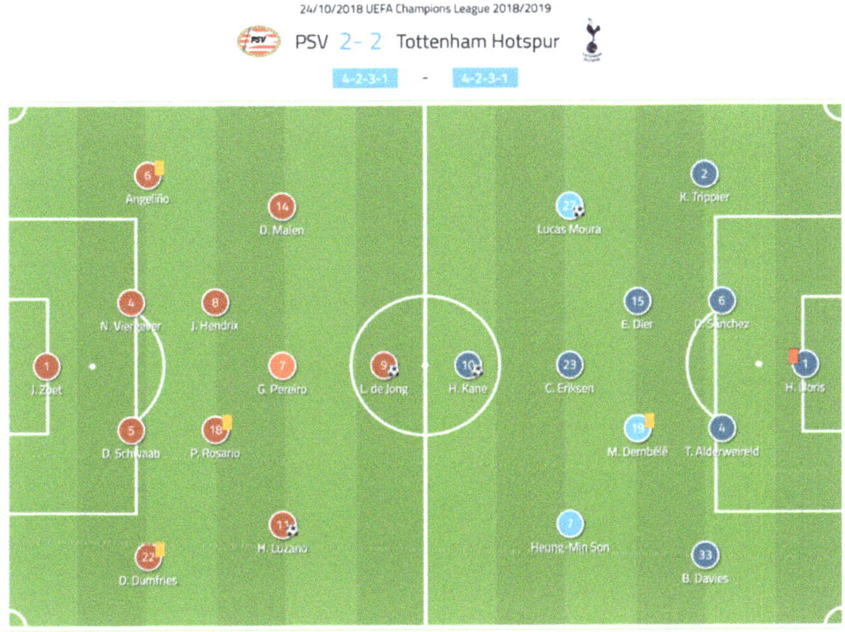

Analyzing the situation

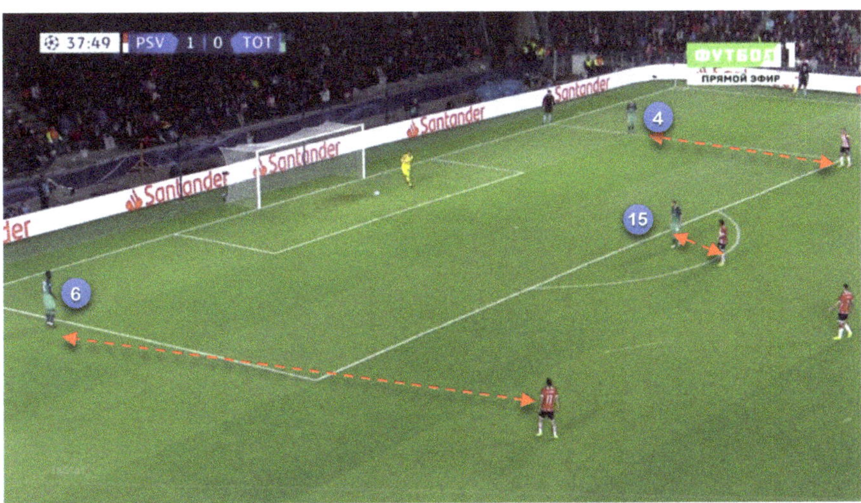

Tottenham sets up to play short in their normal structure: Open centerbacks (4 and 6) and one of the center midfielders (15) dropped back. PSV places their right winger (14) closer to Alderweireld (4), while their left winger (11) is positioned farther away from Sánchez (6), inviting the goalkeeper Lloris (1) to play to his right centerback (6) so that they can pressure him.

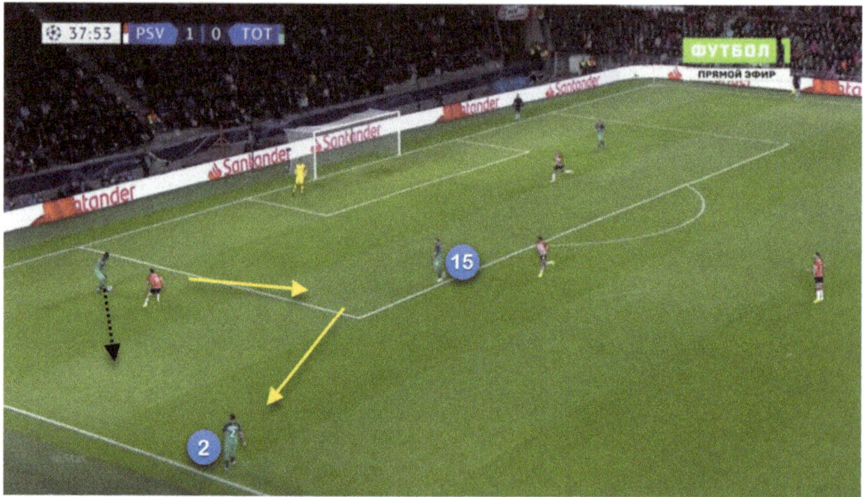

When the left winger moves to pressure Sánchez (6), it opens up the right fullback (2), who was his initial marking reference. However, this passing line is blocked by the body position of the player who was marking the opposing winger. Sánchez could use the support of the right center midfielder Dier (15) as the third man, in order to find the fullback (2). Instead, he decides to resolve the situation with an individual action, overcoming the winger's marking and playing a pass to the fullback (2).

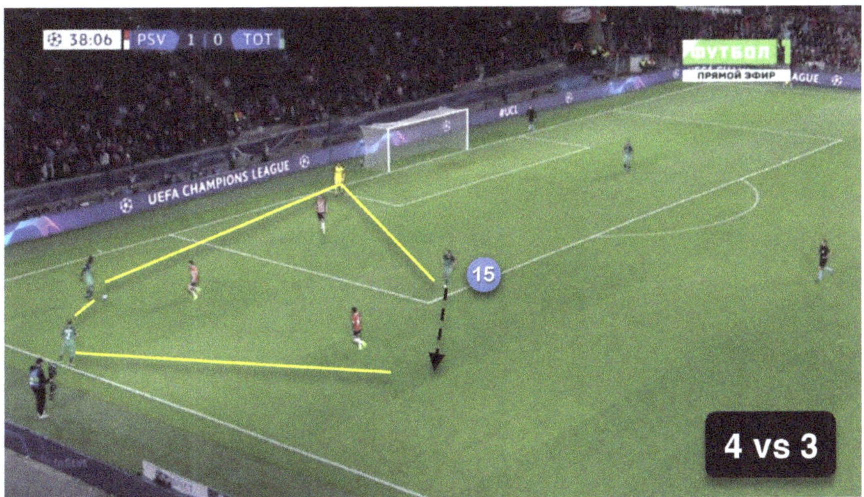

This produces a sequence of passes in that section of the field, generating a numerical superiority of 4 v 3 in Tottenham's favor that allows them to escape the opponent's pressure. Good positioning, distances between the players, and reading of the space.

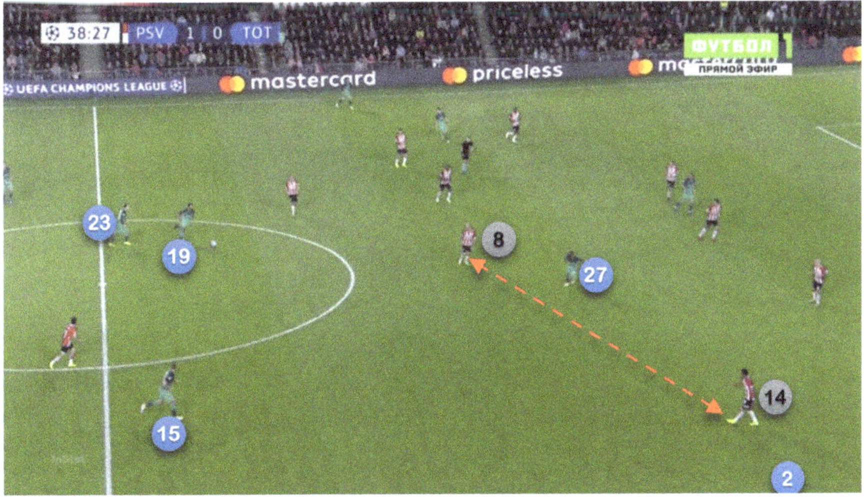

As Tottenham progresses down the left side, we see that the right winger Lucas Moura (27) narrows his position to look for a better location for a pass between the lines. The high position and the width of the right fullback, Trippier (2) creates width between the fullback and (14) and the right center midfielder of PSV.

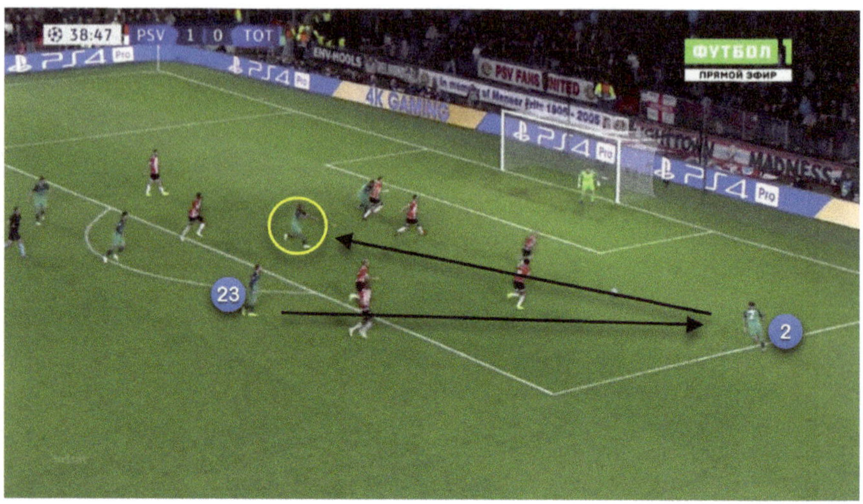

The attacking midfielder Eriksen (23) turns to reposition himself and receives between the lines. He quickly play a deep pass for the right fullback, Trippier (2), who cuts the ball back to Moura (27). Goal for Tottenham.

PROGRESSION - FINISHING

Situation 1: the cutback cross

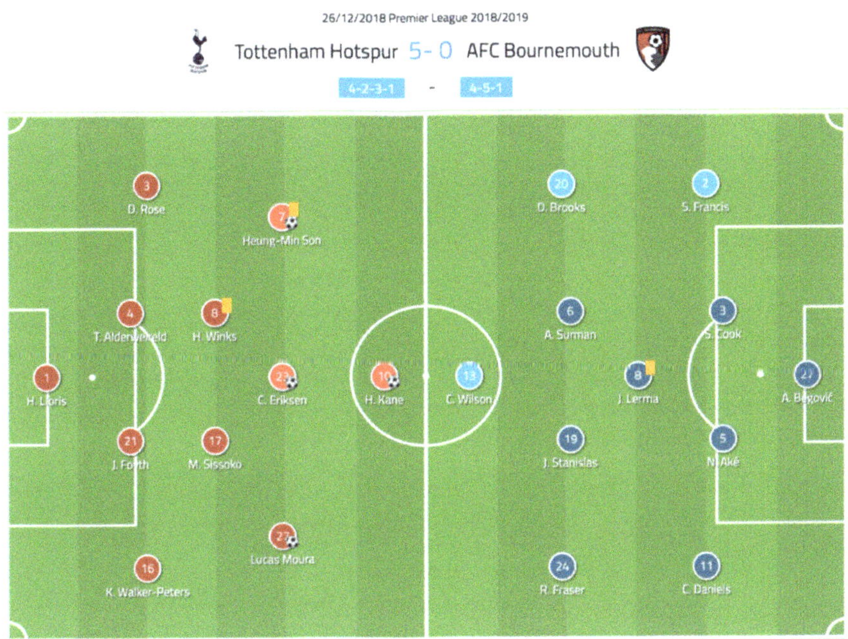

Analyzing the situation

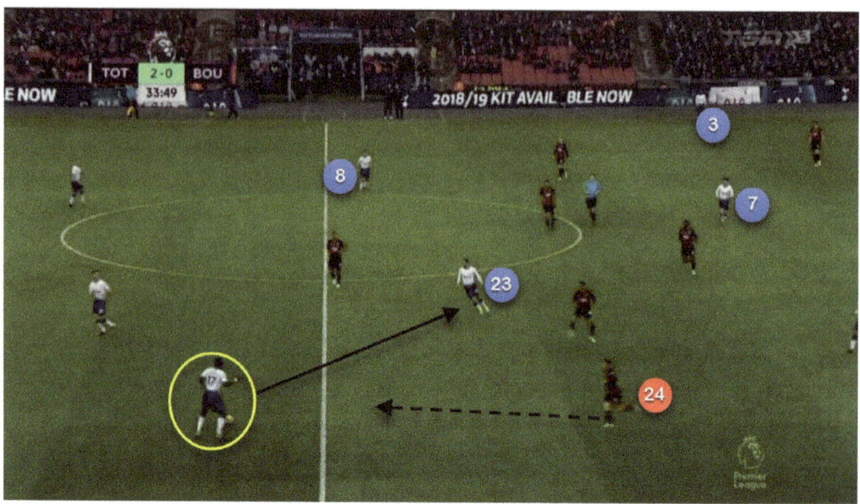

With the ball under control and the opponent's defense compact in their own half, the right center midfielder Sissoko (17) sits back on the right side. Not only does this make him a passing option, it also provides depth for the right fullback (16) who is opening up and the winger (27) who is tucking in so as not to occupy the same attacking channel.

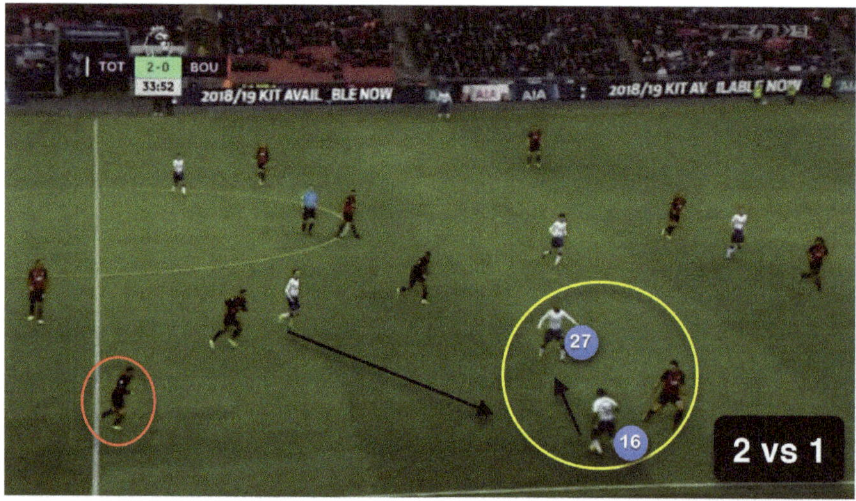

The position of Sissoko (17) prompts the winger (24) to pressure him, leaving a 2 v 1 behind his back with the left fullback (11). Eriksen (23) plays one touch to the right wing (16), who plays to Moura (27).

There is a defensive reorganization that prevents Tottenham from progressing, so they decide to play backwards. The wingers (27 and 7) move inside and the fullbacks (16 and 3) move out wide. Walker-Peters (16), after his intervention, recovers his position along the back line. Sissoko (17) passes to the right centerback (21), who plays short to the left center midfielder (8).

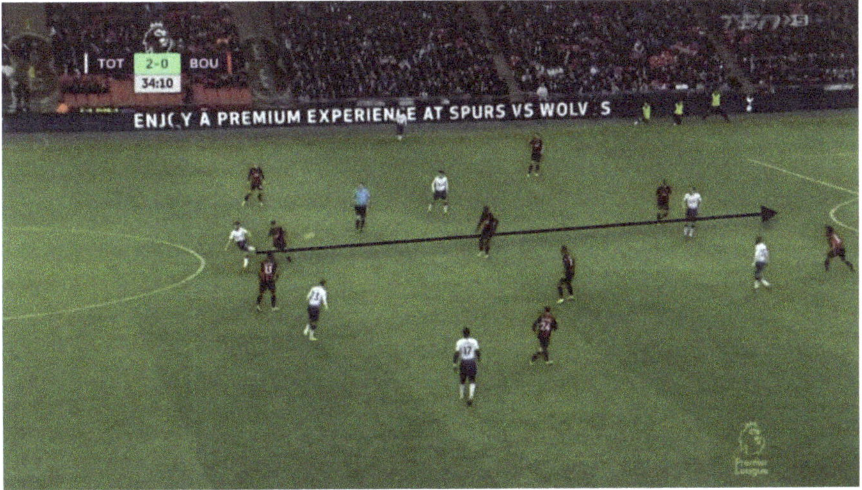

Tottenham's right fullback dismarks behind the back of the opposing left centerback (11) and receives a long pass from the left center midfielder (8).

Moura, who was positioned between the lines, arrives alone facing the goal to receive a cutback pass from the right fullback (16). The run of center forward Kane (10) into the middle of the penalty area drags the two centerbacks with him, which frees up his team mate (27). Goal for Tottenham.

Situation 2: attacking the space

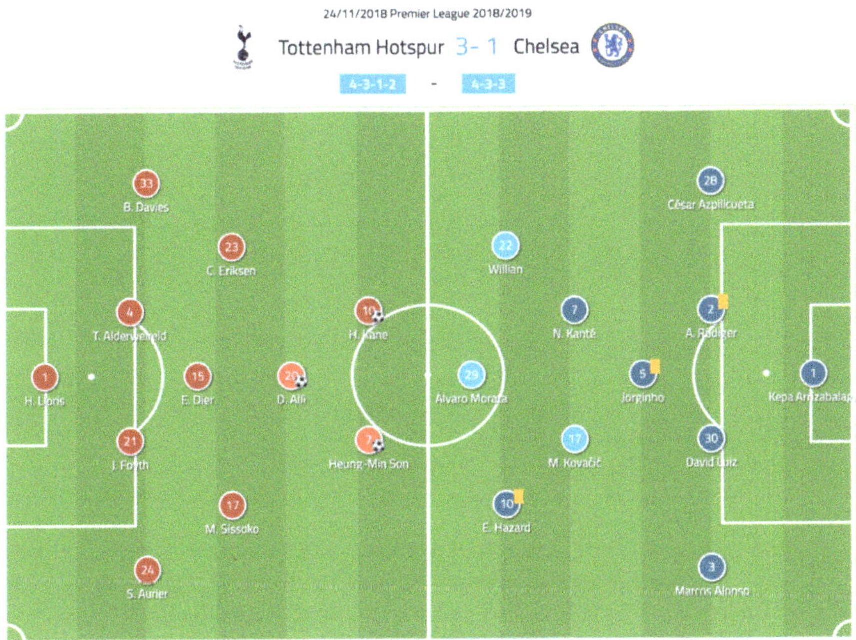

Analyzing the situation

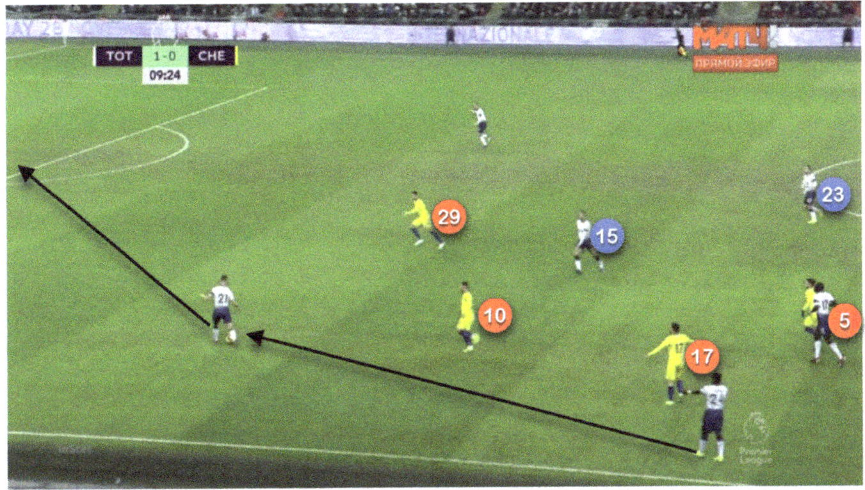

With the ball almost at the midfield line, Tottenham are pressed and decide to turn back and play to their goalkeeper Lloris. Chelsea takes advantage of this situation to push their lines up and continue pressing.

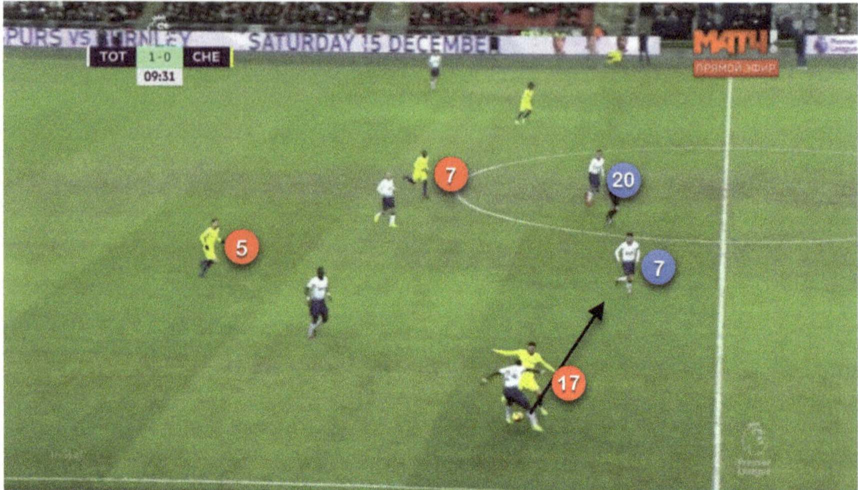

As the pressure from Chelsea continues, Lloris finds the right fullback (24) who is pressed by the left center midfielder (17), because the left winger Eden Hazard (10) went to press the right centerback (21). We can see that Chelsea's three midfielders (7, 5, and 17) stay very high, especially the defensive midfielder Jorginho (5). Son (7) and Dele Alli (20) remain free, between the lines.

Son (7) receives and carries the play towards the left side of the field, playing to the left centerback (4), who provides width and plays to the left

fullback (33). The center forward Kane (10) dismarks to the outside, which drags the right centerback (2) with him. The attacking midfielder Dele Alli (20) positions himself in the center forward spot, which pins David Luiz (30). This produces space between the centerbacks that Son (7) uses to receive the ball, control, and turn.

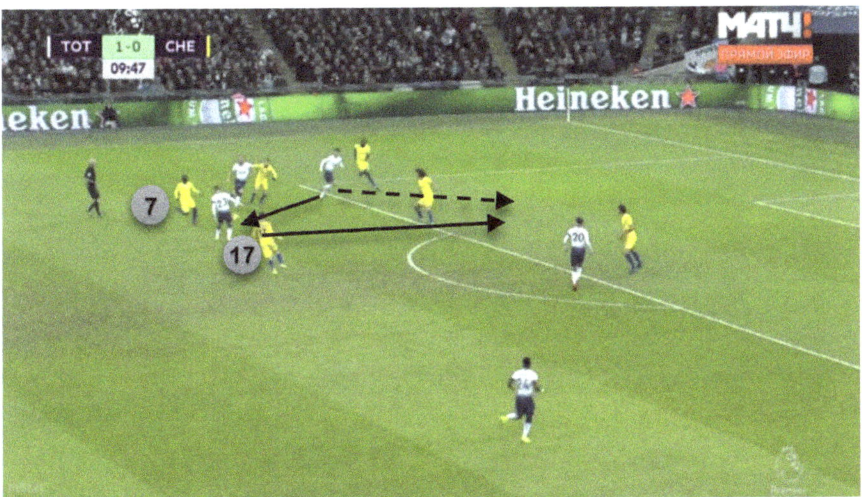

The defensive midfeilder Jorginho (5) goes to press Son (7), which leaves Eriksen (23) unmarked. Meanwhile, the center midfielders of Chelsea (7 and 17) have remained too far away to be able to intervene. Son (7) plays a wall pass with Eriksen (23), who is not blocked by any opposing defender and is left with a clear scoring chance.

Situation 3: the forward drops down

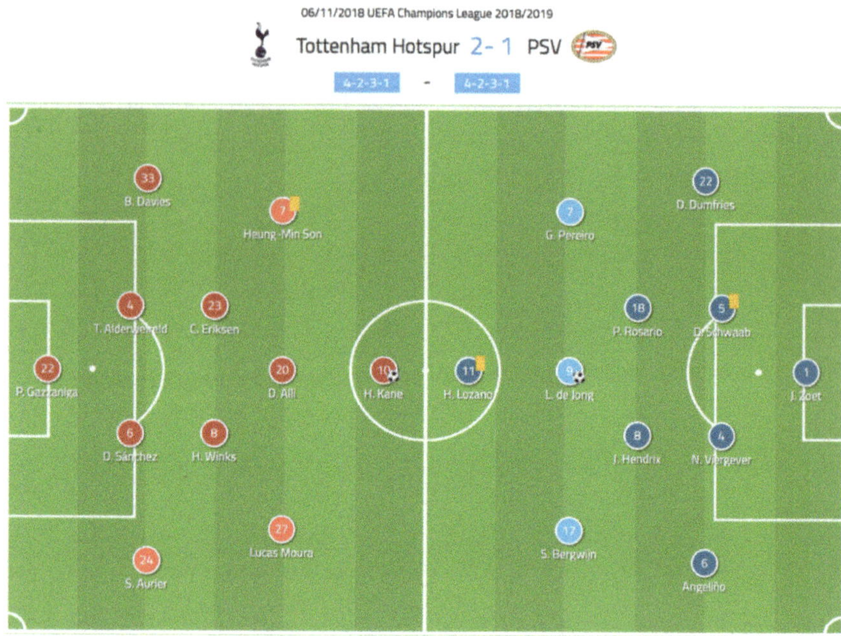

Analyzing the situation

With the ball under the centerback's control and the opponent playing compact with their lines together, Tottenham mobilizes to find passing options that will allow them to progress.

The left centerback (4) advances with the ball, with the two center midfielders (8 and 23) positioned on a diagonal, maintaining good body profiles in case they are able to receive the ball. The center forward Kane (10) drops down to offer himself as a passing option in the central zone.

This action by Kane (10) drags his marker, the right centerback (5), with him. The attacking midfielder Dele Alli (20), who was positioned on the left section of the field, makes a diagonal run forwards towards the space that has been created, controls the ball, and shoots on goal. Dele Alli (20) initiates the pass from the left centerback (4) by starting the run towards the opponent's penalty area.

FORWARDS BETWEEN THE LINES

A center forward can drop back from his starting position near the two centerbacks in order to receive between the opponent's midfield and defensive lines. While this is happening, the center forward will be followed by one of the centerbacks, which will generate space that can be occupied by another team mate. If the opposing centerback decides not to follow him because an opponent could occupy that space, the center forward will be able to receive the ball unmarked.

Situation 4: after a diagonal run – a straight run

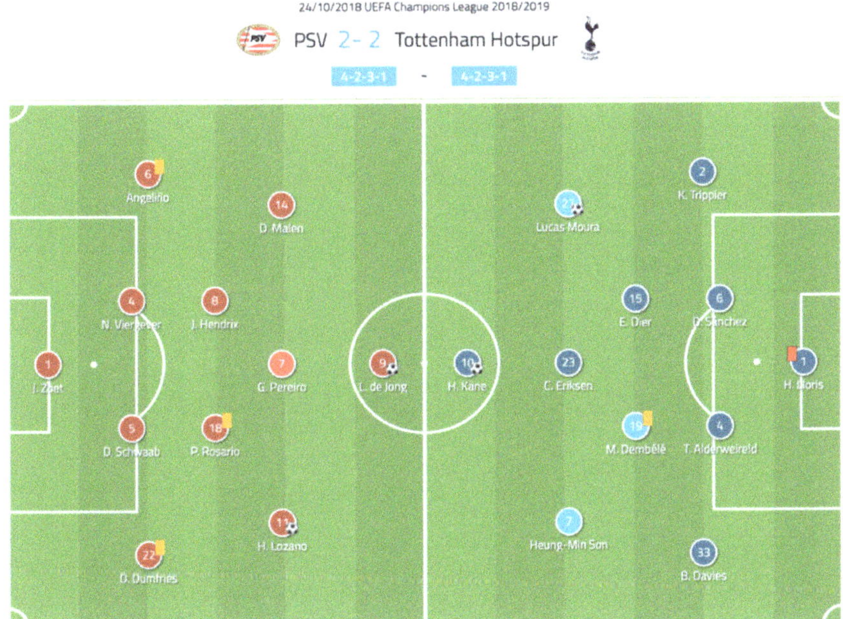

Analyzing the situation

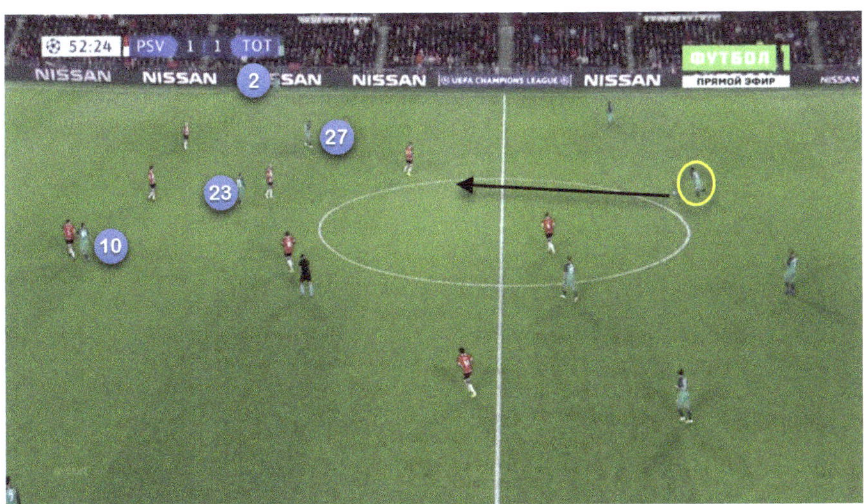

Tottenham is in progression, with left center midfielder Dembelé carrying the ball forward through the central zone. The right fullback (2) finds himself out wide, while the right winger (27) is tucked in.

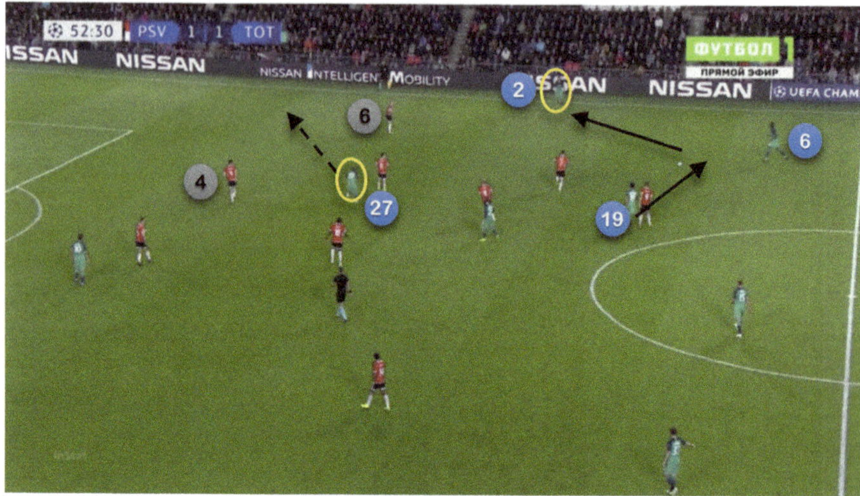

Dembelé (19) cannot find a clear forward pass to break lines. Confronted by the rival attacking midfielder (7), he plays to his own right centerback (6).

Because of advanced positioning of the right fullback (2) the opposing left fullback (6) is unsure whether to mark him or not. Moura (27) cuts from inside, makes a diagonal run behind the back of the left fullback (6).

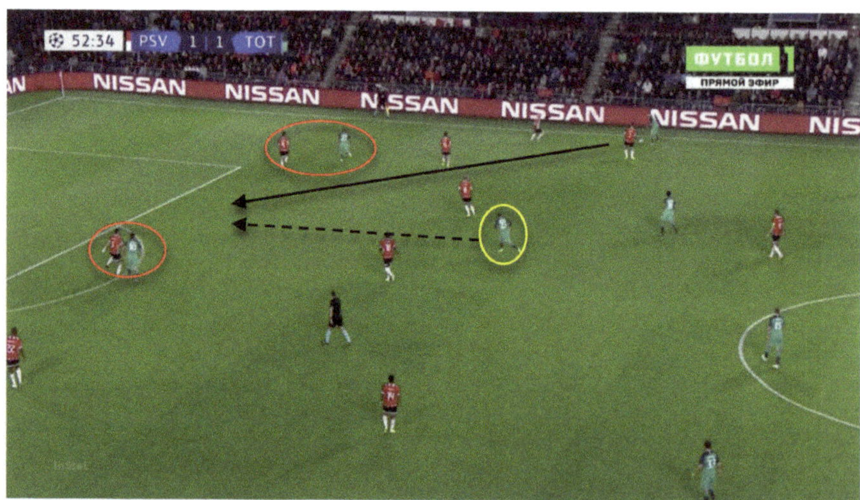

This movement by Moura (27) provokes the left centerback (4) to move

to the outside. The center forward Kane (10) pins the right centerback (5), which leaves space and distance between the centerbacks. The attacking midfielder Eriksen (23) accelerates in a straight line in order to become an option in this space.

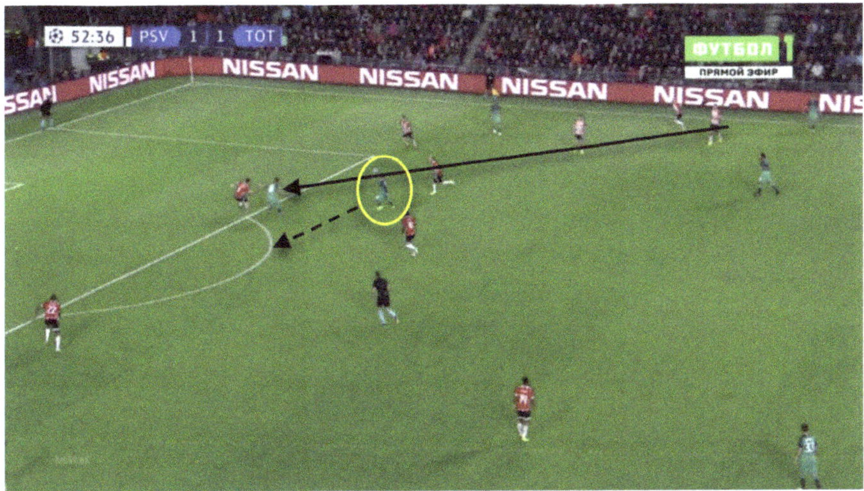

The right fullback Trippier (2) plays a pass into the space, which is free of markers. Kane (10) goes in search of the pass, but sees Eriksen (23) arriving alone and unmarked in the area and leaves the ball for him. Goal scoring situation.

AFTER A DIAGONAL PASS, A STRAIGHT PASS

An extract from the book *Fútbol sin trampa*, where César Luis Menotti explains this concept: "In the case of the diagonal run... I get tired of seeing the center forwards getting the ball. They are at the edge of the area and moving to the side, towards one of the corners, pursued by their marker, naturally (they are in the finishing zone). Then you see that they are given the ball in a position that is totally inappropriate for receiving it, because they have their back to the goal, with a marker behind them, and are limited by their proximity to the sideline. This forward, who has made a diagonal run, isn't doing it to receive the ball, but to be a distraction. Behind his back, in a straight line, another team mate needs to appear.

Situation 5: forwards, midfielders – midfielders, forwards

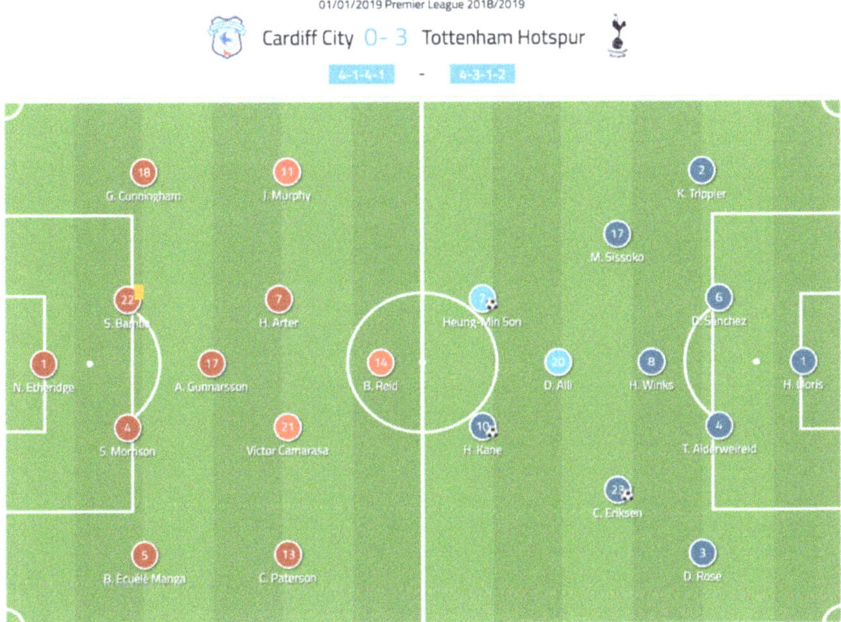

Analyzing the situation

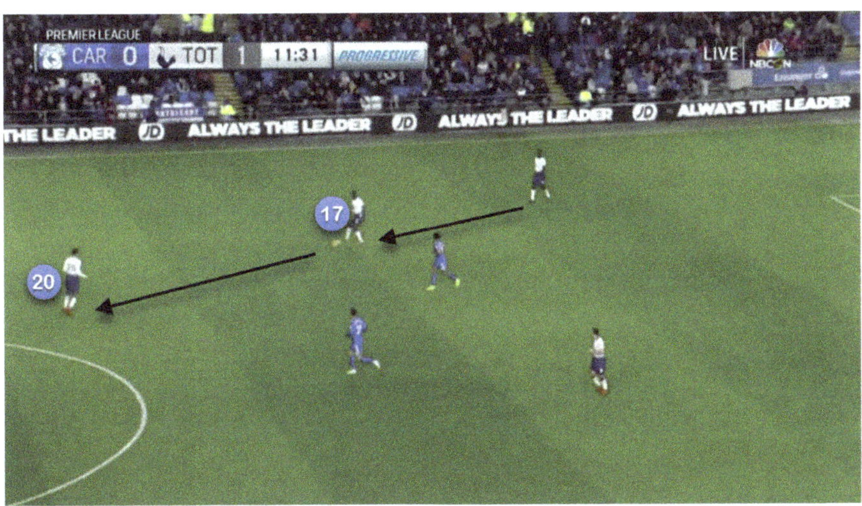

In the starting zone, the attacking midfielder Dele Alli (20) drops to be an option for the right center midfielder Sissoko (17). With time and space, Dele Alli turns and faces forward.

Sissoko continues his run on the right wing. The right fullback Trippier (2), who finds himself deep in Cardiff's half, drops back and drags the marking fullback (18) with him. This has drawn both the opposing fullback (18) and winger (11) to the ball.

Now the center forward Kane (10) drops down, and Dele Alli (20) plays to him, and Kane plays one touch into space for Sissoko (17) to receive. Kane's movement draws out one of the centerbacks (4).

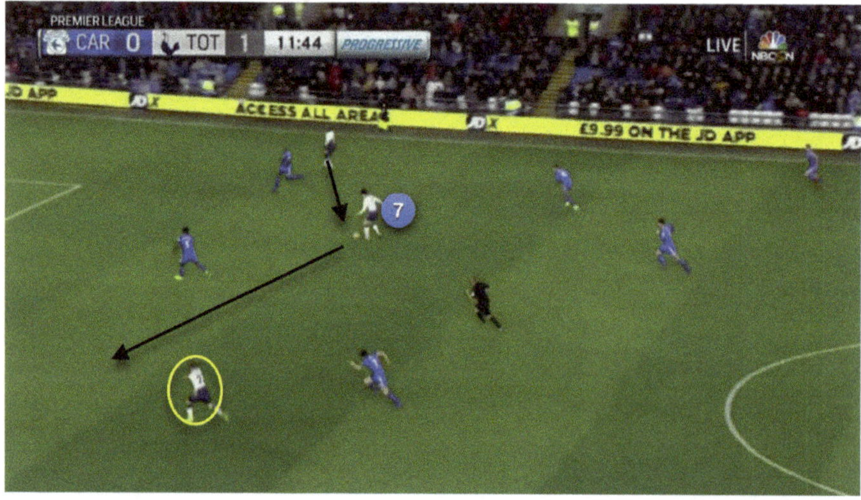

The left centerback (22) goes to prevent the cross, which forces the right back (5) to close in rapidly. The second forward Son (7), who was between the lines, receives a pass from Sissoko (17) and plays quickly to Eriksen (23). Eriksen maintains his position, receives the pass, is pressured, takes a touch, and converts the chance. Goal for Tottenham. A goal by a midfielder that was started by a forward.

OFFENSIVE DISORDER - INTERPRETATION
When a team has players who can rotate positions in the offensive phase, can interpret the moments and the areas of the field, can combine together, and can execute all this in the correct way, it's a huge advantage for disorganizing the opposing team.

CHAPTER 4

KLOPP

INTRODUCTION

USUAL SYSTEM OF PLAY. USED IN 60% OF THE GAMES.

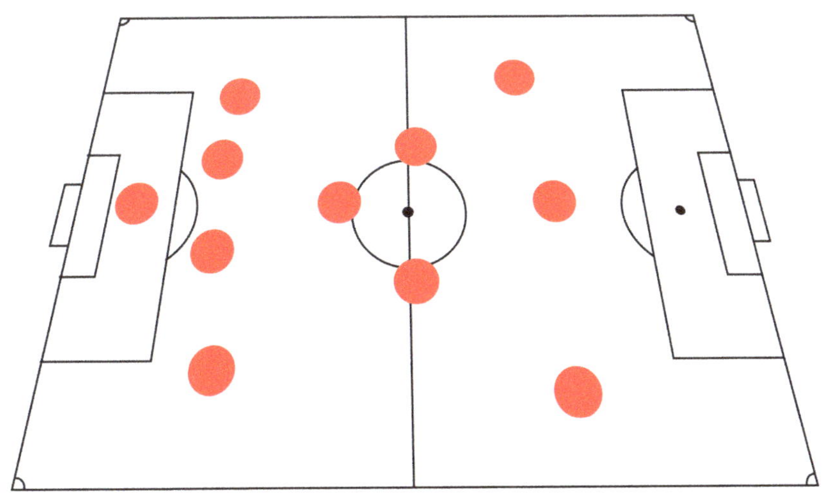

1-4-3-3

Key points to Klopp's attacking organization

- Passing quickly into the opponent's half of the field
- Changing the point of attack
- Long passes
- Occupying space
- Attacking fullbacks
- Offensive disorder through the wingers
- Individual superiorities

BUILDING OUT THROUGH THE GOAL KICK

Situation 1: playing out short – under high pressure

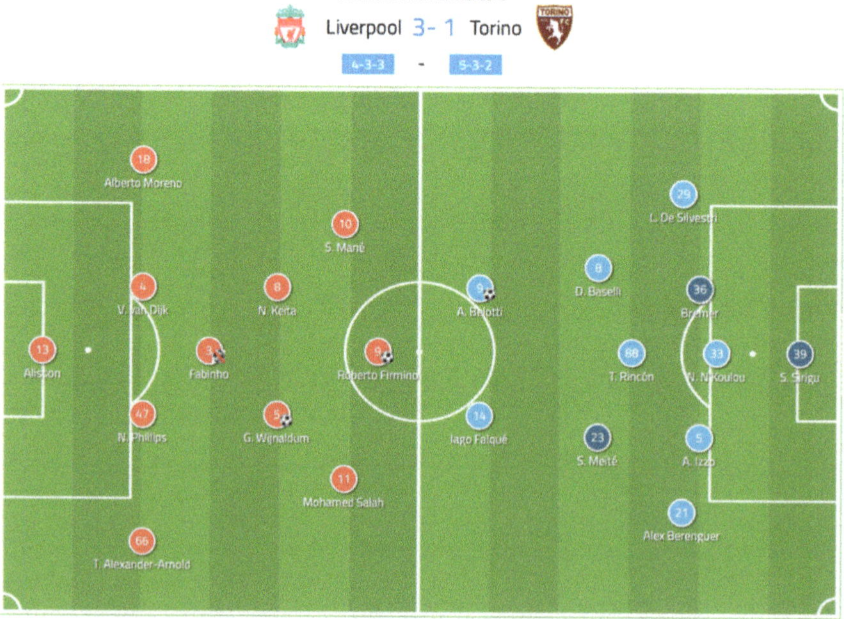

Analyzing the situation

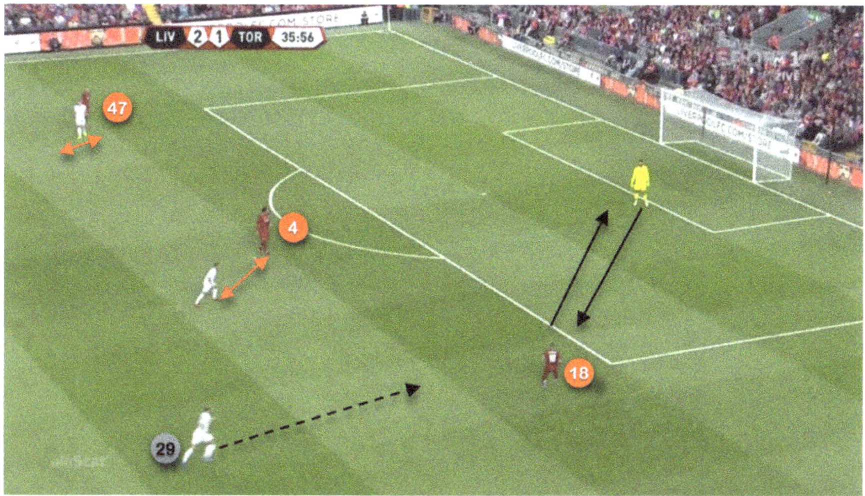

Liverpool arranges a line of three players close to the ball, with 2 centerbacks (47 and 4) plus the left fullback (18) who has dropped down. The goalkeeper Alisson (13) plays quickly to the left fullback, who receives facing his goal and returns the ball to the goalkeeper due to the pressure from the opponent (29).

Faced with the continued pressure from Torino, Alisson (1) controls the ball and launches a long direct pass to the right winger (11) on the opposite side of the field from where the play started. None of Liverpool's midfielders

drew near to Alisson to offer a short passing option, however all of them can be found close enough to win any possible knock-on generated by Salah (11).

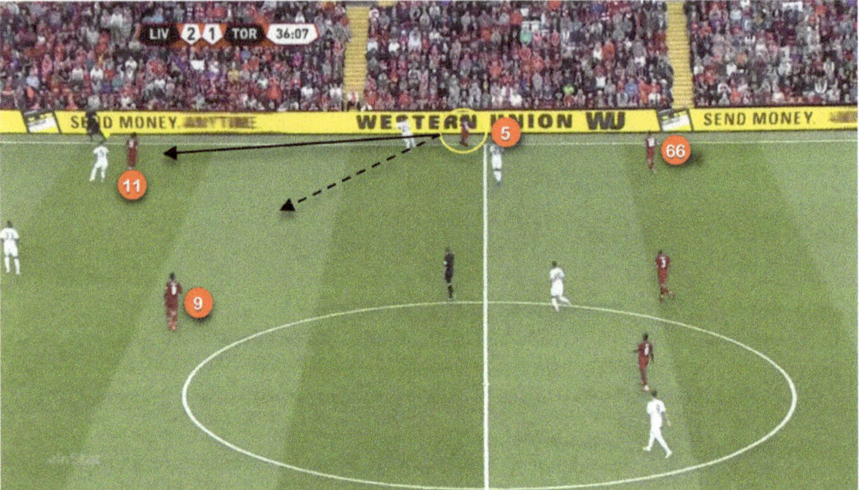

Salah (11) drops the ball down towards the right center midfielder (5), who makes a one touch pass and runs forward, eliminating his marker. He receives the ball from Salah again and continues running with the ball. The center forward Firmino (9) moves to the center and the left wing Mané (10) moves to the opposite side.

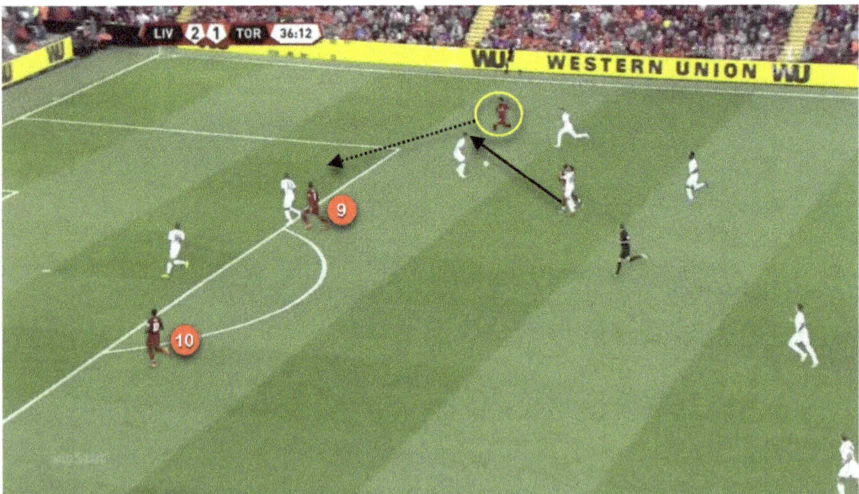

There is a clear intention to attack quickly. The right center midfielder Wijnaldum (5) runs with the ball and returns a pass to Salah (11), who enters the penalty area to attempt a finish on goal. Goal scoring situation.

PREESTABLISHED OPTIONS WHEN FACED BY AN OPPONENT'S SPECIFIC BEHAVIOR

It is important to define the anticipated manner in which our team will behave when faced with the specific actions of the opponent. "When faced with opposing pressure when playing out short, I should launch a long pass to the opposite side" (the example we just analyzed).

In this situation we can see that the three midfielders know that the goalkeeper, faced with continuous pressure from the opponent, will play long to the opposite side from where the ball came. So these players will be nearby in order to support and win the ball. We have to make it clear when the midfielders should come close to the ball and when they shouldn't.

Situation 2: centerback under pressure – change of zone

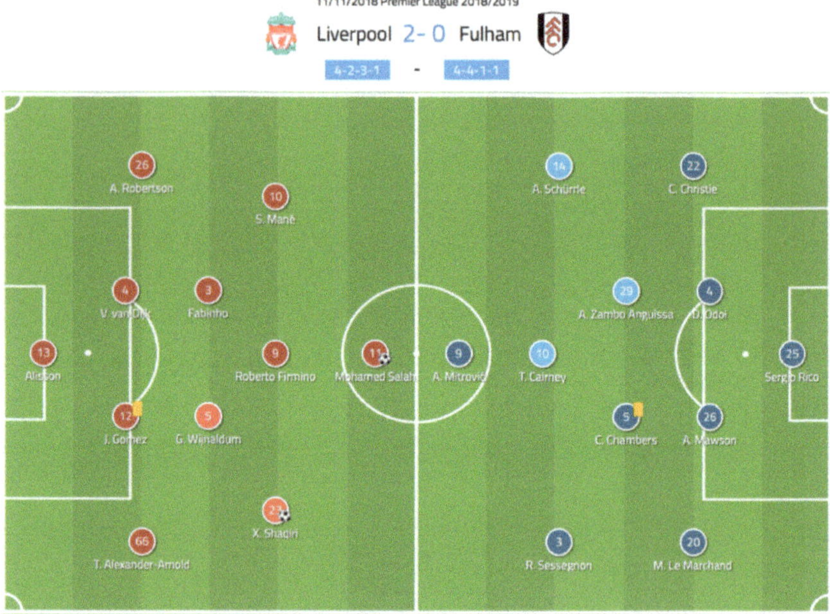

Analyzing the situation

Liverpool is playing out short with the right centerback (12) Pressured by Fulham's center forward (9), Gomez plays back to the goalkeeper Alisson (1). The opposing 9 continues to pressure the ball.

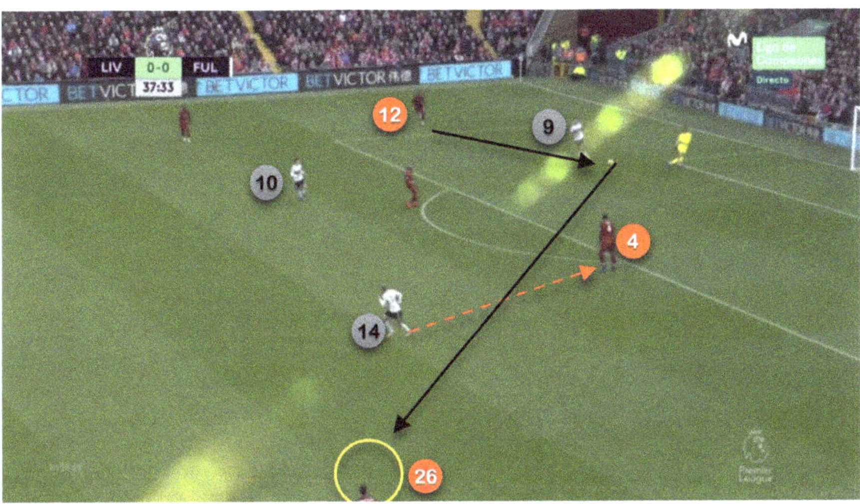

Since Fulham's left winger (14) is on top of Liverpool's left centerback (4), the left fullback (26) appears as a free passing option for the goalkeeper (1), because Fulham does not change their marking references.

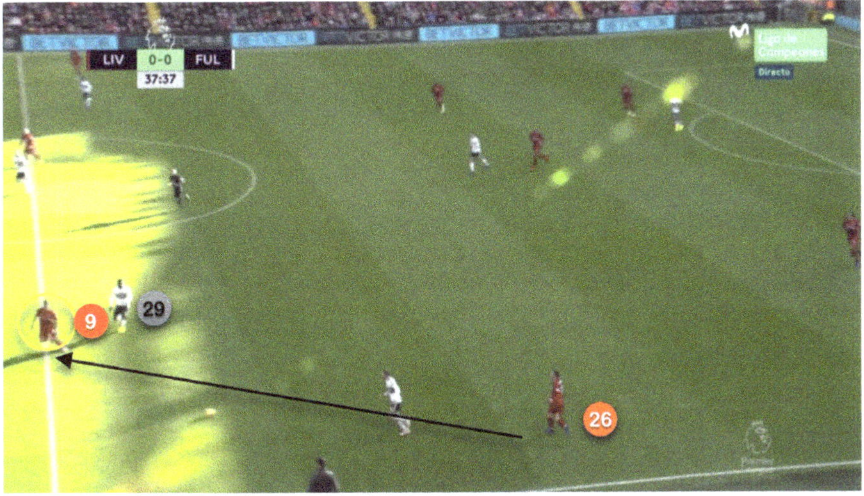

The left fullback Robertson (26) receives with time to control the ball and take it forward. The attacking midfielder Firmino (9) dismarks to break the line, behind the back of the right centerback (29).

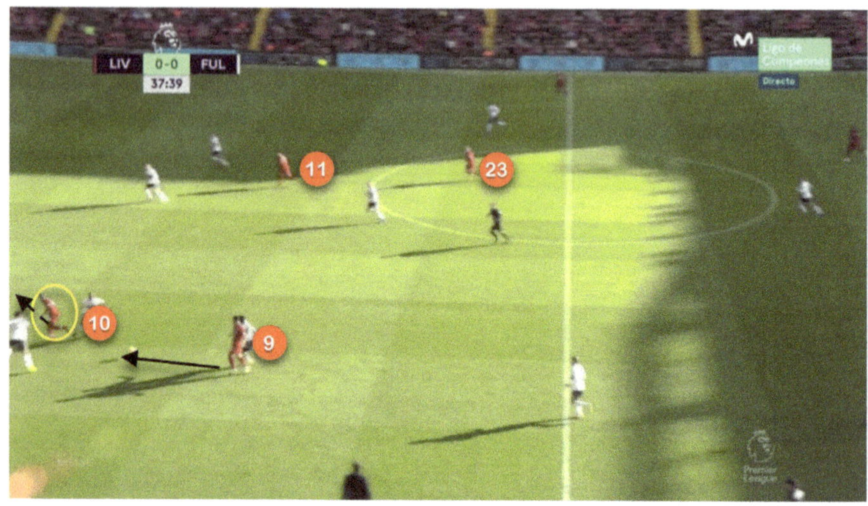

Firmino (9) receives the ball going forward and plays quickly to the left winger Mané (10), who dismarks into depth behind the last line and into space, in order to enter the area with the ball under control.

WITH SPACE, DISMARKING TO BREAK LINES

When we are faced with a team that has considerable space between their lines, dismarkings to break lines becomes an option. These are produced behind the back of the opponent's closest line, playing quick and vertical forward passes, without giving the opponent time to regroup defensively. For this action we need both players who can read the game quickly and move forward, and players capable of making those vertical passes that break lines at the right moment.

Situation 3: buildout through the centerback – opponent positioned high

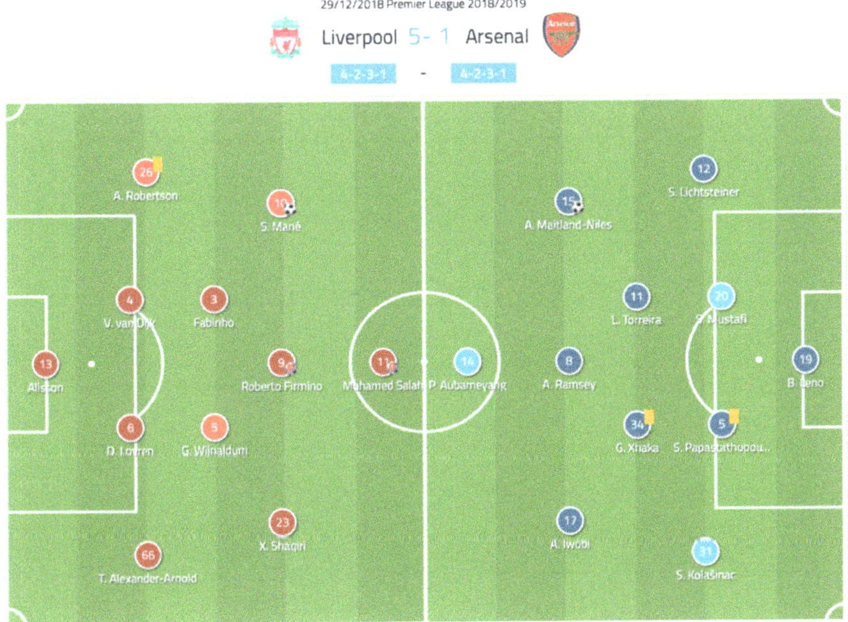

Analyzing the situation

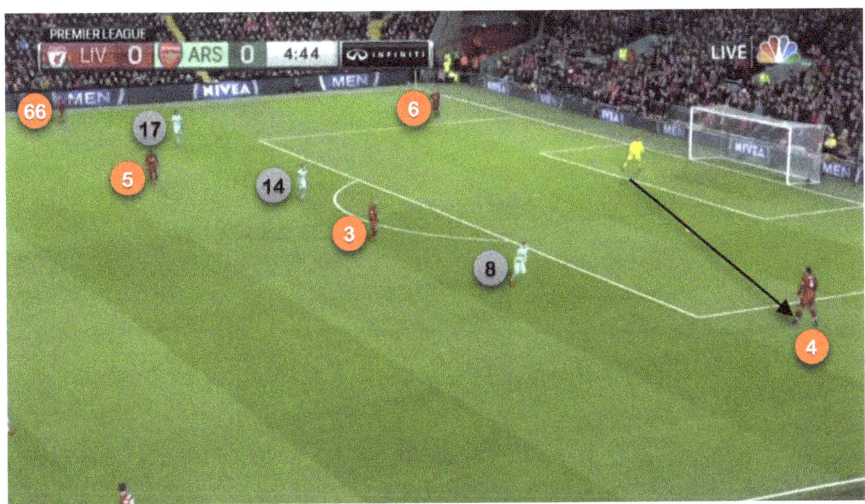

Arsenal takes up a high position with three players: center forward (14), attacking midfielder (8), and left winger (17). Alisson (1) plays to the left centerback (4), who controls the ball but does not shape his body to play forward, so he plays it back to the goalkeeper.

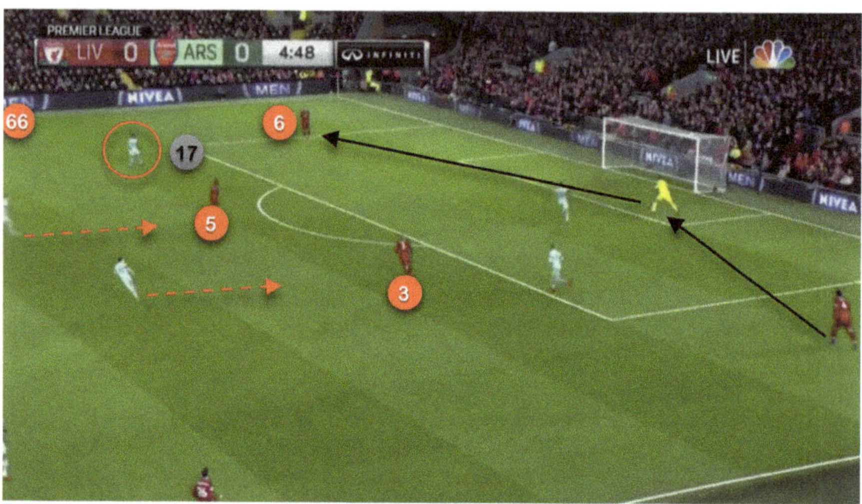

Arsenal intensifies the pressure and closes down the goalkeeper, while the left winger (17) remains in an intermediate position between the centerback (6) and the right fullback (66), taking into account Liverpool's tendency to play through the opposite side of the field with the fullback. This positioning of the opposing 17 gives Alisson (1) time to play to the right centerback.

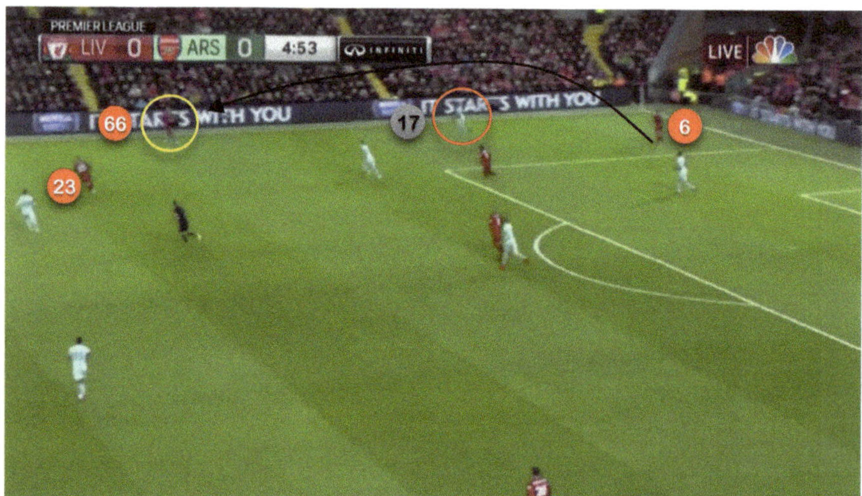

The left winger (17) pressures the right centerback (6), blocking the passing line to the right fullback (66), but he plays forward anyway. The fullback (66) touches the ball forward and plays to the right winger Shaquiri (23), who is acting as an option inside.

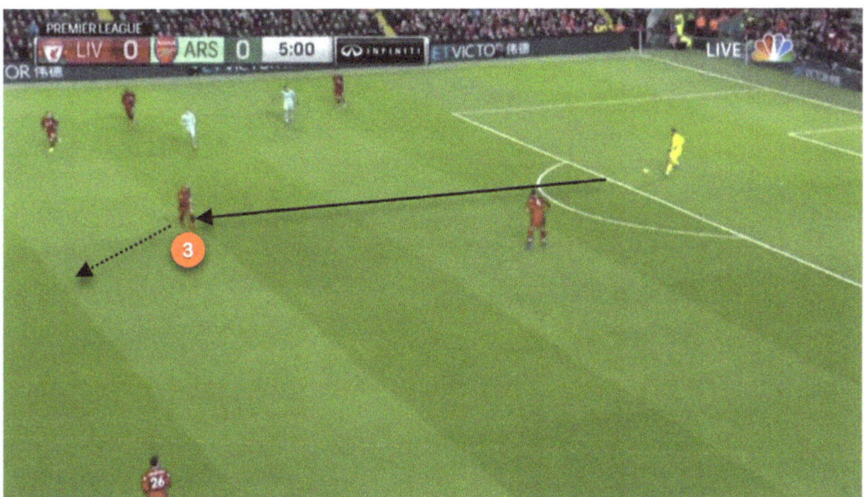

Shaquiri (23) relieves the pressure by playing back to the goalkeeper. In this way, Liverpool reorganizes their positional attack to have more time and space.

PROGRESSION - FINISHING

Situation 1: diagonal run inside from the opposite wing

Analyzing the situation

Faced with the opponents defending in a compact 4-4-2 in their own half, Liverpool's centerbacks (6 and 4) are carrying the ball with space and time. The player who decides to speed up the play with a vertical pass is Lovren (6), the right centerback.

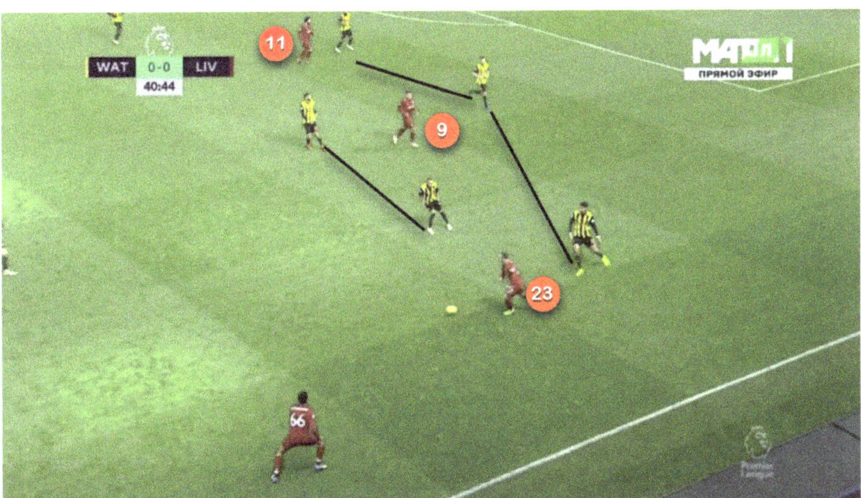

The pass is for the right winger Shaquiri (23), who dismarks diagonally inside. Watford maintains their two lines of four. The position of the attacking midfielder Firmino (9) forces the left centerback (15) to continue marking him. The same happens with Salah (11), who is being watched nearby by the right centerback (6). This produces a 2 v 2.

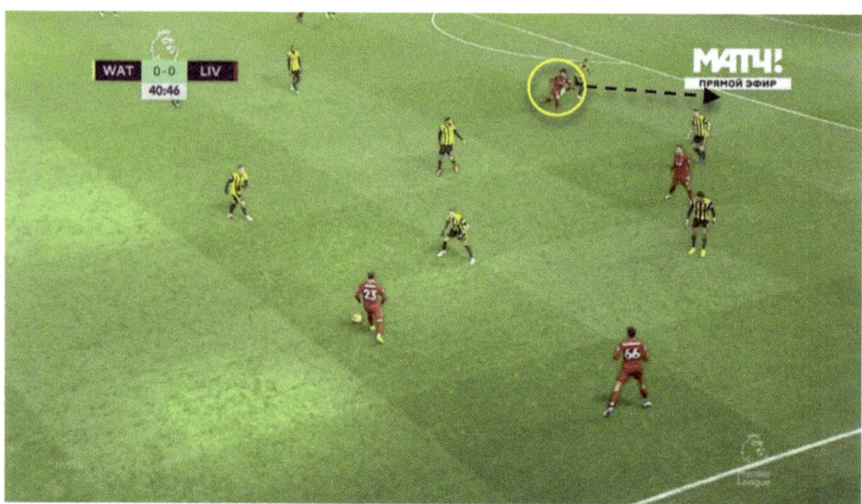

Playing inverted, Shaquiri (23) goes inside. Salah (11) shows for a diagonal pass behind the back of the left centerback (15), a movement that forces the marker to follow him in case the ball is played to this area.

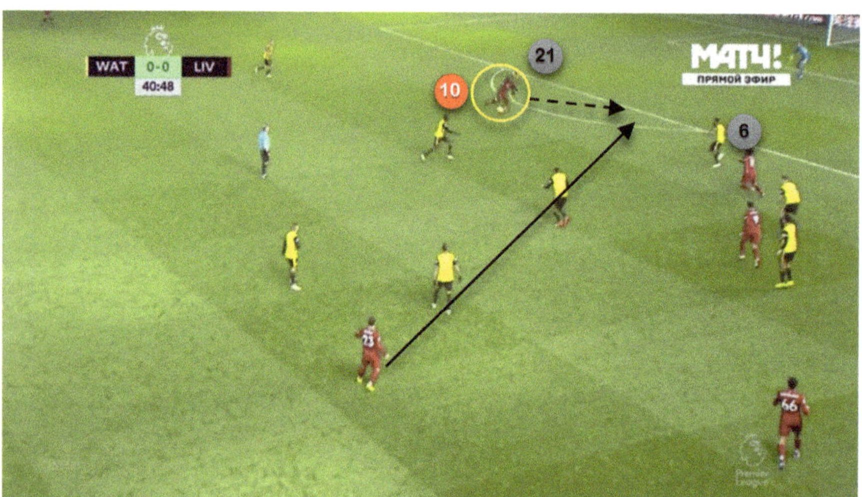

This creates space between the right centerback (6) and the right fullback (21), which is exploited by the dismarking of the left winger Mané (10), who started the attack by pinning his marker out wide but then appeared inside to be an option at the right time. He controls the ball in the area and shoots on goal.

Situation 2: enter - exit - enter

Analyzing the situation

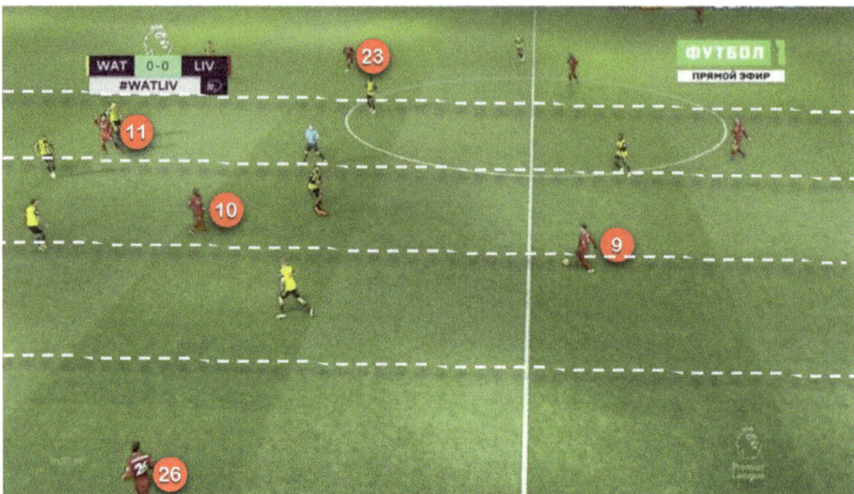

During the start of play, the left centerback Van Dijk (4) plays to the left fullback Robertson (26), who finds himself unmarked and is then pressed high by the right winger (19). The first passing option that he has is the attacking midfielder Firmino (9), who has dropped back. He plays to (9) and Watford reorganizes quickly into their 4-4-2. The Liverpool player all occupy different channels.

The left winger Mané (10), appearing as usual as an option inside and between the lines, leaves the left wing in order to make room for the fullback to move forward. Watford closes the inside spaces well and leaves the outside spaces free. Firmino (9) does not play to Sané (10), who drops back to offer an option, and decides to play to Robertson (26) instead, because he can play with more time and space. The left fullback (26) lightly attracts the opposing right fullback (21), while Mané (10) turns from inside to dismark towards the wing.

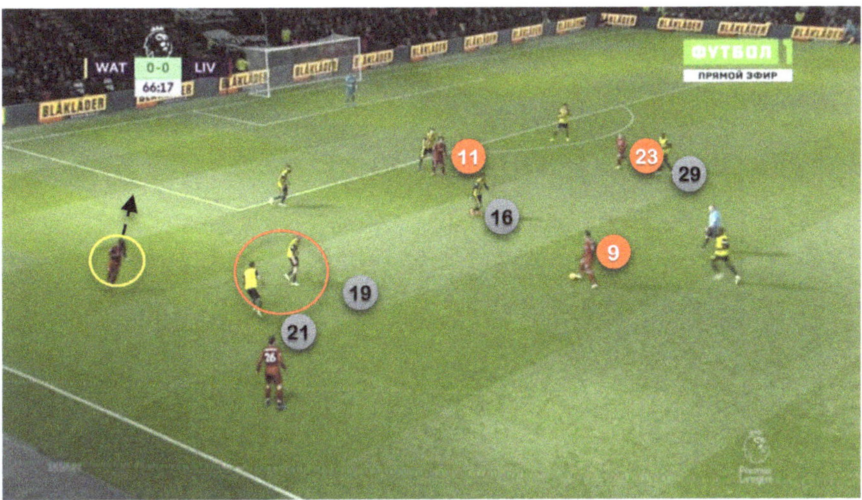

This collection of movements leaves the fullback (21) and the right winger (19) disorganized. Robertson (26) plays to Firmino (9), who continues to offer support from behind the line of the ball. The center midfielders of Watford (16 and 19) remain organized, facing Firmino, but without going to pressure.

Mané (10) takes advantage of the disorganization of the fullback (21) and the winger (19) to receive in depth from Firmino (9). He controls the ball and passes to Salah (11), who finally converts the chance into a goal.

Situation 3: from fullback to fullback

Analyzing the situation

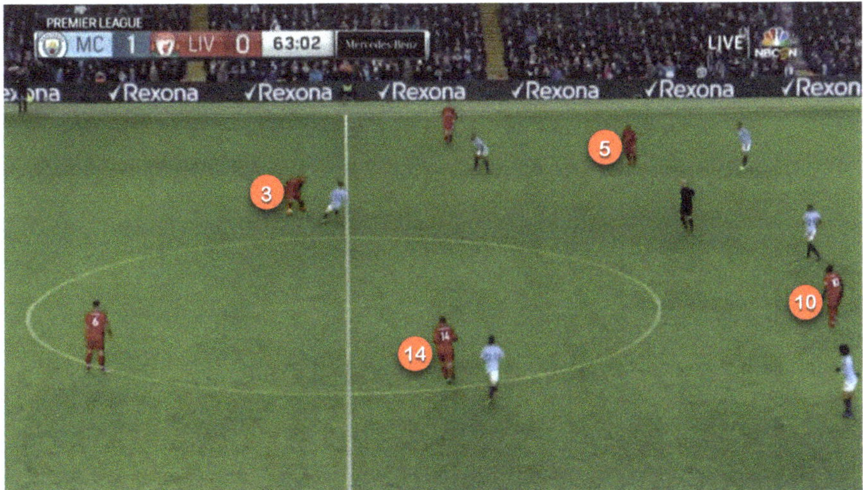

Liverpool changes their starting tactical system, moving to a 4-4-1-1 with Fabinho (3) and Henderson (14) as center midfielders, Wijnaldum (5) as left winger, Mané (10) as right winger, Firmino (9) as attacking midfielder, and Salah (11) as center forward. Being unable to progress, Fabinho (3) opts for a switch of play to Firmino (9) by launching a long pass to another part of the field.

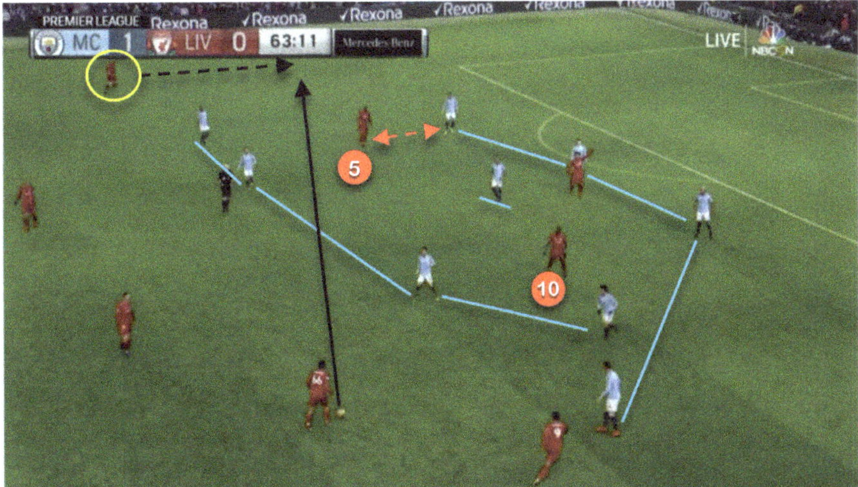

The switch of play gives Manchester City time to shift and reorganize into their defensive 4-1-4-1 shape. Firmino (9) controls the ball and plays

to the supporting right back (66). The position of the wingers, especially that of Wijnaldum (5), pins the opposing right back (3). This prompts a switch of play from fullback (66) to fullback (26).

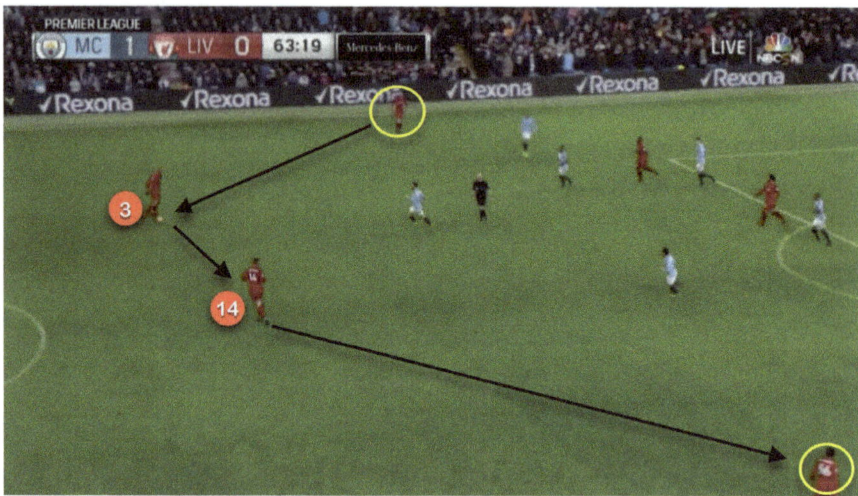

Robertson (26) controls the pass from Alexander-Arnold (66), while City moves quickly to this side of the field to curb any possibility of progression. Liverpool's center midfielders (3 and 14) offer support. Fabinho (3) plays to Henderson (14), who turns to open up the game on the right wing through the right fullback (66). Liverpool once again changes the direction of the attack from left to right.

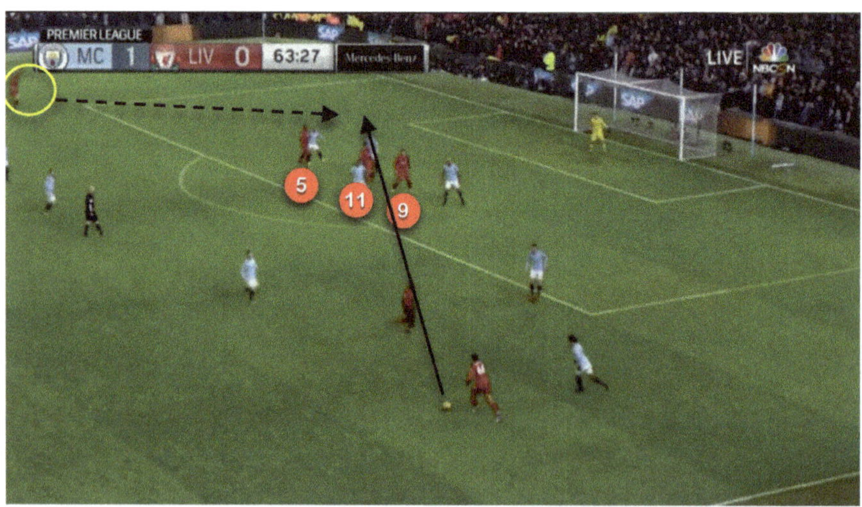

Alexander-Arnold (66) uses a feint to get past his opponent, left winger Sané (19), and crosses the ball behind the right fullback Danilo (3), so that the opposite fullback Robertson (26) can arrive without the ball. We see that City has a 4 v 3 numerical advantage in this area. The arrival of the left fullback (26) from behind surprises the opponent, whose touch to Firmino (9) helps him convert the chance into a goal.

SWITCHING PLAY

There are attacking situations in with the opponent confronts us with an organized defense, rapid defensive shifting, and takes away the space between the lines to prevent playing inside. The ability to switch play requires players inside to pin the opponents and players outside to give width to the team, which will force the opposing team to start moving. During these movements, in the moment when a bad individual or collective decision is made by the opponent, advantageous spaces will be generated that will allow progression.

Situation 4: play vertical and attack

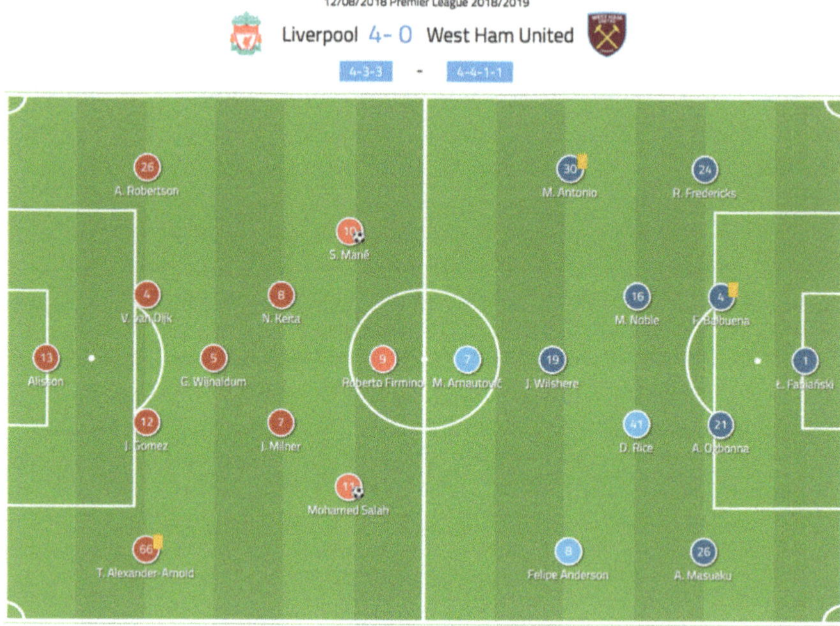

Analyzing the situation

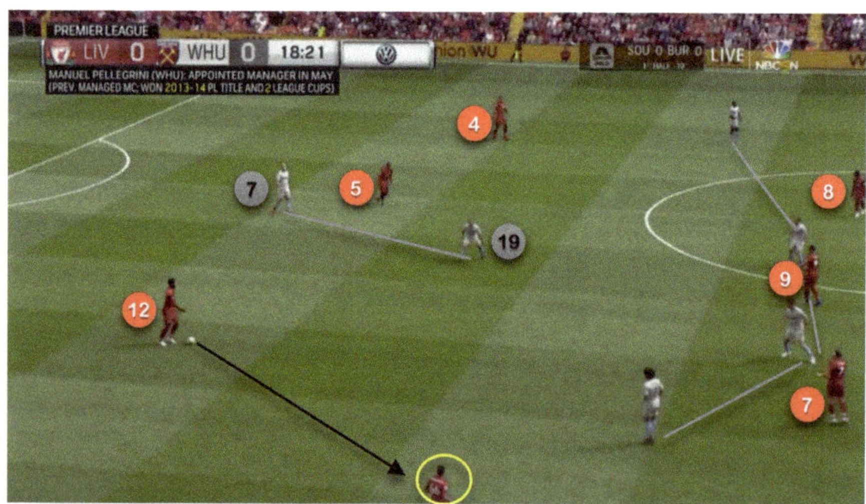

The right centerback Gomez (12) is in possession of the ball. West Ham presents a 4-4-1-1 defensive organization. The insertion of Wijnaldum (5) between the centerbacks means that the center forward (7) is watching him attentively to prevent a progression through him. However, two West Ham players (7 and 19) oppose a single Liverpool player (5), which allows the right centerback (12) to play with more time and space.

Gomez (12) plays to the right fullback (66) Alexander-Arnold. When Alexander-Arnold receives the ball and positions his body to play forward, the right center midfielder Milner (7) moves towards the wing to show himself as a passing option, which prompts that opposing left center midfielder (41), who has been marking him closely, to follow. This creates an imbalance in the distances between West Ham's center midfielders.

Keita (18), the left center midfielder of Liverpool, recognizes the empty space that has been generated, and dismarks in a diagonal behind the back of both opposing center midfielders in order to receive the ball unmarked and facing forward towards the opposing goal.

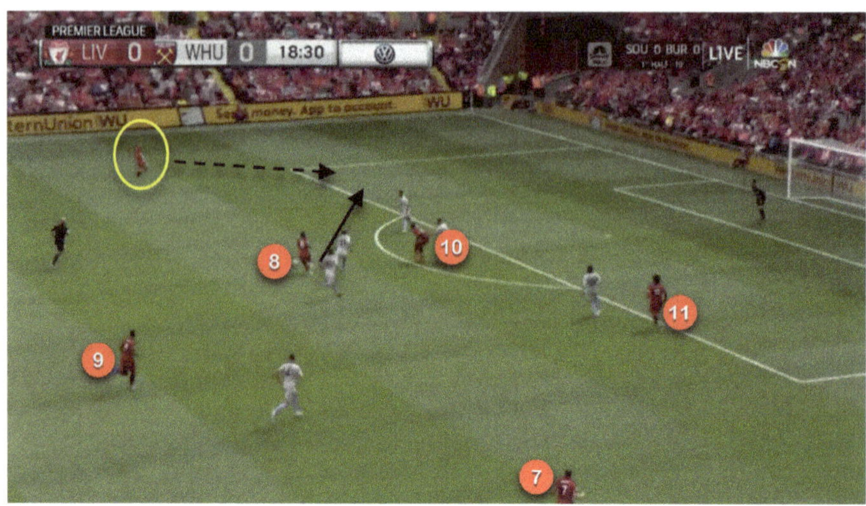

Keita (8) runs with the ball enough to attract and pin the opposing defenders, and this also allows him to buy time for the left fullback (26) to join the attack and put in a low cross. The width that is always maintained by Liverpool's fullbacks, as well as their physical abilities, allows them to always appear as an extra option for the resolution of the team's attacks.

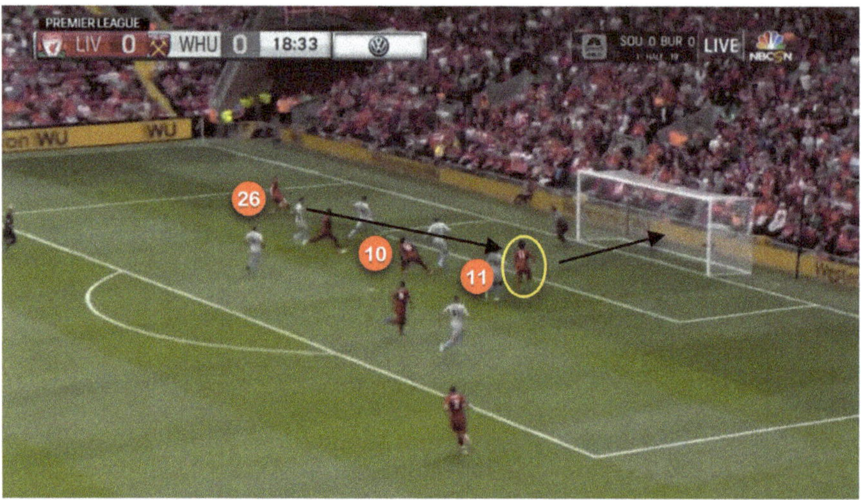

Robertson (26) makes the best possible decision; a first time pass into the middle of the area. The center forward Firmino (9) isn't there because he participated in the start of the movement as a passing option, but the two wingers Mané (10) and Salah (11) find themselves in a position to finish the action. Goal for Liverpool.

ALWAYS IN THE AREA

There are center forwards who often get wide, drop down, and participate in the management of the game. If the play progresses in a rapid and vertical way, this is not going to give the center forward time to arrive in the area. For this reason, the team needs to occupy the penalty area with players who will be positioned as references in the places where they want to put the ball (near post, the center of the goal, far post) in order to increase the likelihood of a proper finish to the attack.

Situation 5: individual superiority

Analyzing the situation

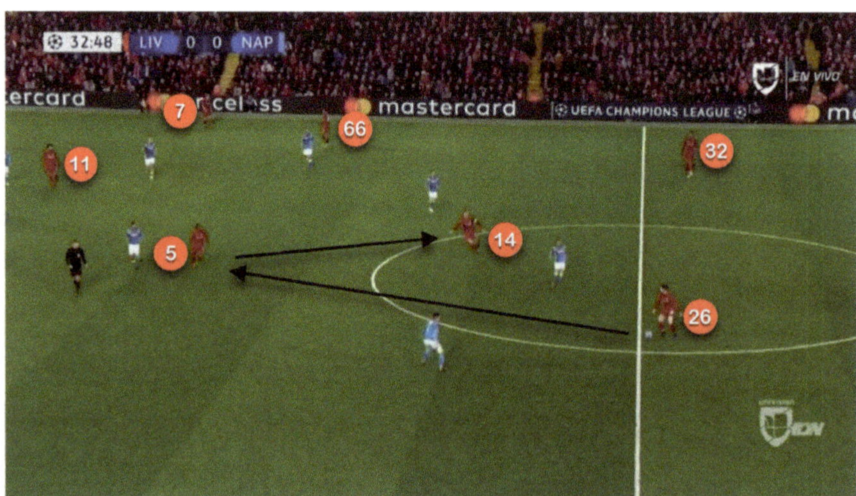

The ball is in possession of the left fullback Robertson (26) in the middle of the field. The entire opposing team is in their own half, obstructing any clear passing options. Because of this, the concept of the third man appears, as Robertson (26) plays to one of his center midfielders (5), who then plays to the supporting defensive midfielder (14) who is facing forward.

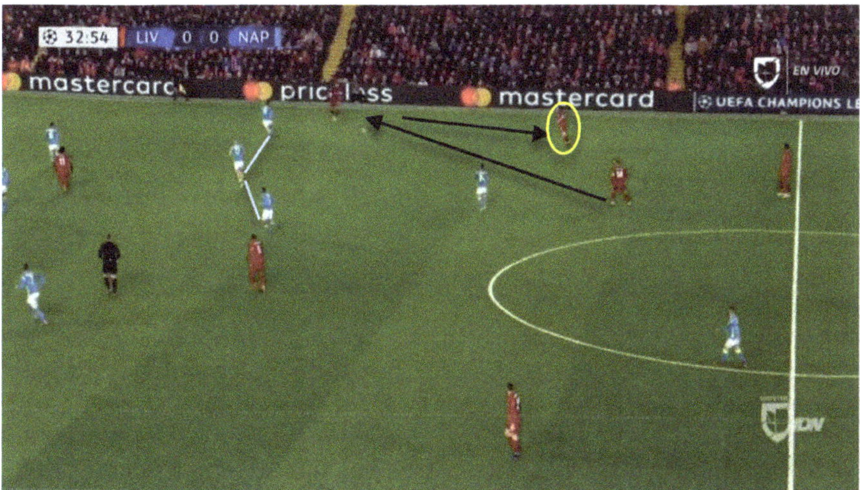

The play has opened up on the right wing with the fullback (66), who is maintaining the width. Napoli shifts and closes down the spaces for progression, while one of the center midfielders (7) appears as a support behind the line of the ball. Since he does not find space, Milner (7) decides to play back to the right centerback (32). The opponent is well organized defensively.

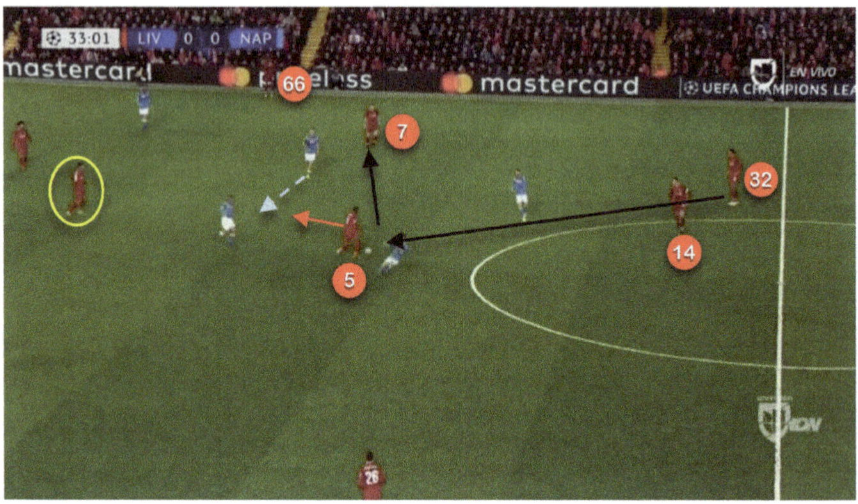

The right center midfielder, Wijnaldum (5) appears as an option between the midfield and forward lines. Here he receives a pass from the right centerback (32), controlling the ball with his body profiled to play forward to Milner (7). The center forward Firmino (9) drops back and prompts the center midfielders of Napoli (4 and 17) to close the spaces in order to prevent a pass inside to him. This free up Milner (7).

With two touches, Milner (7) controls the ball moving forward and then plays a pass inside to Salah (11), which the left center midfielder (17) is unable to cut out, because of the run that he made first to obstruct the interior pass to Firmino (9). The right winger Salah (11) finds himself with his back to goal and marked by the left fullback (6).

After receiving the pass he benefits from the contact with the fullback (6), and is able to turn and enter into a 1 v 1 situation with the left centerback (26). Here, Salah (11) displays all of his individual superiority, leaving the centerback (26) behind, shooting, and converting the chance.

INDIVIDUAL SUPERIORITIES

When we use this term in the world of football, we are usually focusing on the unique ability of each player to resolve situations in the game by making the correct decisions and executing them with the proper technique. When that occurs, it means that we are in the presence of a player who possesses individual superiority.

CHAPTER 5

TRAINING ACTIVITIES

FROM GAME ANALYSIS TO PRACTICE SESSION

CLARIFICATION: all these exercises are extracted directly from the analysis of real game situations.

Dimensions, number of touches per player, number of passes for the team in possession, and rotations: all of these variables will be adjusted by each coach, according to the quality and level of the players at their disposal. Here, I am only proposing activities that progress in complexity, which are adapted from the concepts of the game that we have previously analyzed.

All of the exercises will be carried out with the same structure.

A) Passing circuits, decision making, unopposed or with minimal opposition.

B) Increased opposition, decision making.

C) Increased game realism with the intention of bringing the exercise as close as possible to the reality of competition, organization, dimensions, opposition, and finishing, involving all the phases of the game.

EXERCISES

GOAL KICKS

Exercises from the goal kick / start of play

The objective of these exercises is to arrive in the opponent's half of the field with the ball under control, by employing the distinct offensive tactical concepts analyzed in the game situations of each coach.

Situations:

1. Buildout through the centerback, progression on the same side.
2. Buildout through the centerback, progression on the opposite side.
3. Buildout through the fullback.
4. Buildout through the long pass.

EXERCISES: GOAL KICKS

Training the situation: building out through the centerback, progression on the same side.

A) Passing pattern – finishing

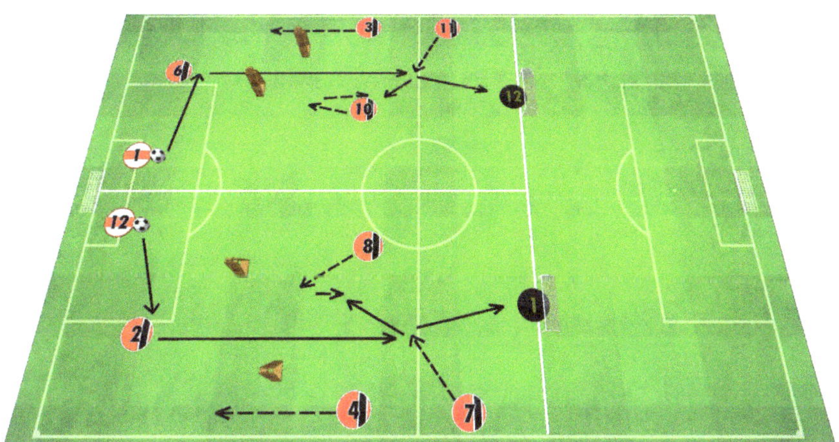

Description: play starts simultaneously from the goalkeepers. Both groups make the same sequence of passes. Example from the left side: the goalkeeper (1) plays to the centerback (6), while the fullback (3) and center midfielder (10) drop down. The winger (11) drops down inside and diagonally towards the space left by the center midfielder (10), so that I can receive a low pass from the centerback (6). Once he receives the ball he plays it to the center midfielder (10), who turns rapidly in order to finish the play with a shot into the goal.

B) Opposition – overcoming the first and second lines of pressure – finishing

Description: start with the two goalkeepers (12 and 1) playing simultaneously, playing to the centerbacks (2 and 6). Now there is a first and second line of opposition. It's a 4v3 situation where the centerback has several options. The players play with freedom of choice, with the objective of having the ball reach the winger (7 and 11) in a direct manner from the centerback (2 and 6) or indirectly through a third man.

C) Increased game realism

Description: the attacking team plays in a 4-3-3 system and the defending team plays in a 2-4-2. The field remains divided lengthwise and

each side plays with a 5v4 +1 (numbers 5 and 9). Both goalkeepers start play to the centerbacks (2 and 6) and the defending team goes to press. The only players who can play in both sections of the field are the 5 and 9. Both of these players have to make the decision about where to go and which sector needs their support. These players may not intervene in the same sector. This means the maximum superiority that can be achieved is a 6v4. The objective is for the ball to start play and finish play on the same side as it was put into play by the goalkeeper.

Training the situation: building out through the centerback, progression through the opposite side.

A) Passing pattern – receiving zone

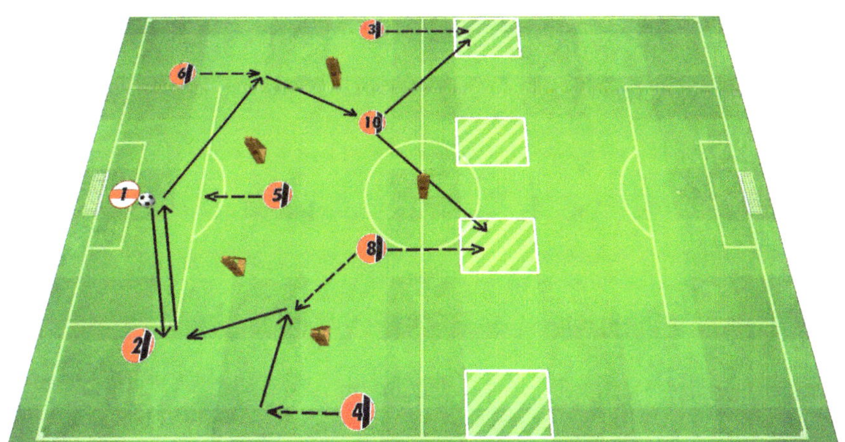

Description: the defenders and midfielders play in a 4-3-3 system. The sequence starts with a pass from the goalkeeper (1) to the centerback (2), while the right back (4) drops down to receive the ball and play one touch to the inside right midfielder (8). This player has also come closer to show in support and plays back to the centerback (2), simulating an inability to progress. The centerback (2) passes back to the goalkeeper (1), who moves play to the left side of the field to the other centerback (6). Then the ball arrives to the feet of the left inside midfielder (10), who touches the ball forward and choses where to play the next pass. Always staying within the area that's been marked out, this player has the left back (3) and the right inside midfielder (8) as options. The next repetition will be initiated on the left side, following the same sequence of passes.

B) Opposition - choosing the best option - reception zone -vertical play

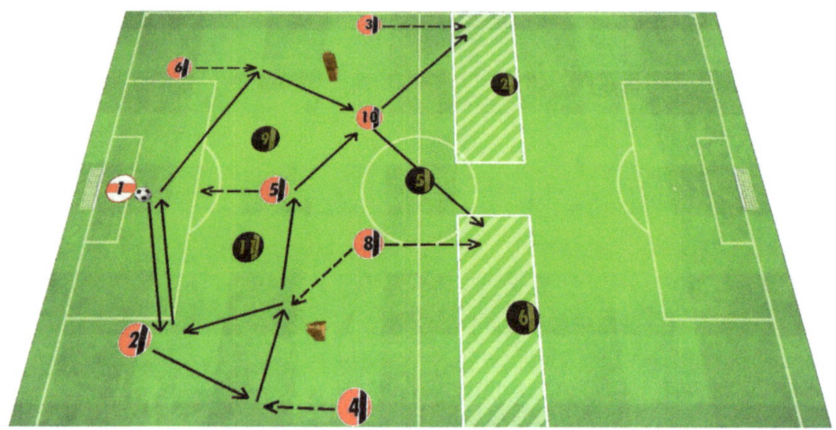

Description: play starts with the goalkeeper (1) to the centerback (2), who is pressured by the forward from the corresponding side (11). As seen in the diagram, the centerback (2) who receives the ball has two passing options (4 and 8). One option is to play the right back (4), who can return the ball back to the centerback (2) so that the play can continue through the opposite side. The other option is to play to the right center midfielder (8), who will also return the ball to the centerback (2) or can find support from the defensive midfielder (5). But in both cases the objective will be to carry the play to the left side.

Once the ball is played to the left centerback (6) or to the left center midfielder (10), it should progress with the intention to make a pass into the zone occupied by an opposing defender (6 or 2).

In this exercise we are looking for decision making and verticality. Play can progress in a 1v1 or a 2v1 (fullback-center midfielder). The defensive midfielder (5) of the opposing team should try to cut out the pass.

C) Increased game realism

Description: Teams play 11 v 10 with 4-3-3 and 3-4-2 systems. Correlate the behaviors of the previous exercises when deciding how to progress and finish through the opposite side.

Training the situation: building out through the fullbacks

A) Passing pattern – accuracy

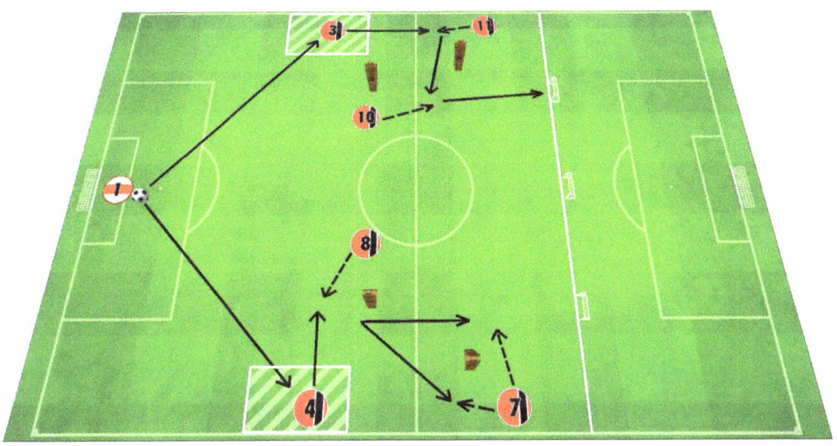

Description: play with the fullbacks (4 and 3), center midfielders (8 and 10) and the two wingers (7 and 11) in a 4-3-3 system. The goalkeeper (1) starts play with a pass to one of the zones where the fullbacks (4 and 3) are stationed. Once they control the ball, both have different options to progress. The right fullback (4) plays to the right center midfielder (8), who drops back diagonally to the same height and plays first time to the right winger (7), who dismarks inside and finishes in the mini goal in the middle.

Another alternative is for the center midfielder (8) to play to the winger (7) who drops down from the wing to do a wall pass that leaves the midfielder (8) facing the mini goal.

In addition, observing the example on the other side, the left fullback (3) plays to the winger (11) who drops down and plays towards the left center midfielder (10), leaving them facing the mini goal in a position to score.

As an option to this last play, the left wing (10) controls the ball and plays to the left center midfielder (10), who gets behind the opponent's back and scores in one of the mini goals.

These four variation are adaptable and can be executed on both sides.

B) Opposition - pressure - decision making

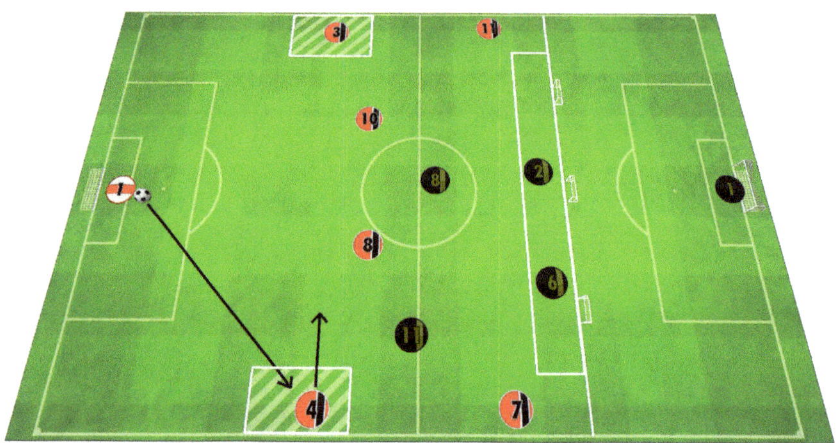

Description: add in four opposing players. Play starts with the right fullback (4), who receives the ball inside the zone shown in the diagram. At that moment the closest opponent (11) needs to decide if he is going to press the fullback or not. The objective is to score in the mini goals that are going to be guarded by two opponents (6 and 2) who cannot leave their zone. The circulation of the ball needs to be quick, so that the defenders don't have time to cover the goals.

C) Increased game realism

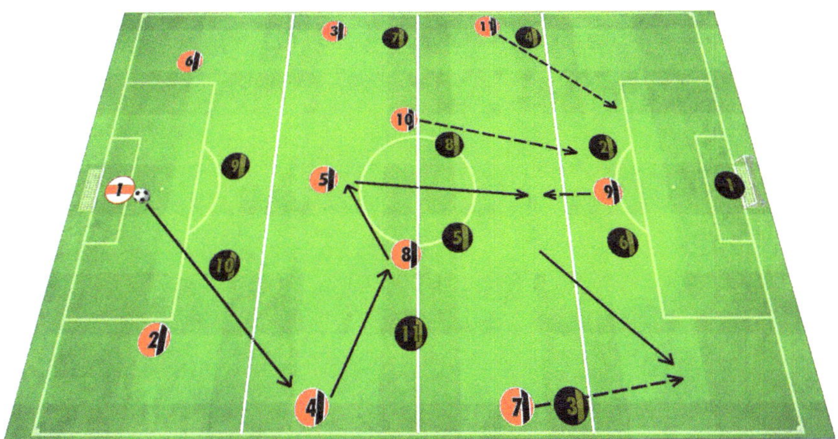

Description: play 11v11 with a 4-3-3 system vs a 4-4-2. There are three zones marked out of the field. The forwards of the opposing team (9 and 10) are not allowed to enter the midfield zone until the moment that the fullback (4) decides to play back to the centerbacks (2 and 6) or the goalkeeper (1). When the fullback (4) controls the ball he will be in the midfield zone in a situation of 7v6 numerical superiority. The center forward (9) of the team in possession can enter the midfield zone to offer a support, while the two opposing centerbacks (2 and 6) may not enter this central zone.

Once the attacking team decides to penetrate, it will be through the wingers (7 and 11) dismarking into space. The opposing fullbacks (4 and 3) are not allowed to follow into their own defensive zone. At least three players (center forward – left center midfielder – left winger) should arrive in the penalty area for the final action, with a maximum of four (right center midfielder). The centerbacks of the opposing team should defend the attack.

Training the situation: buildout through the long pass

A) Organization – second ball areas – finishing

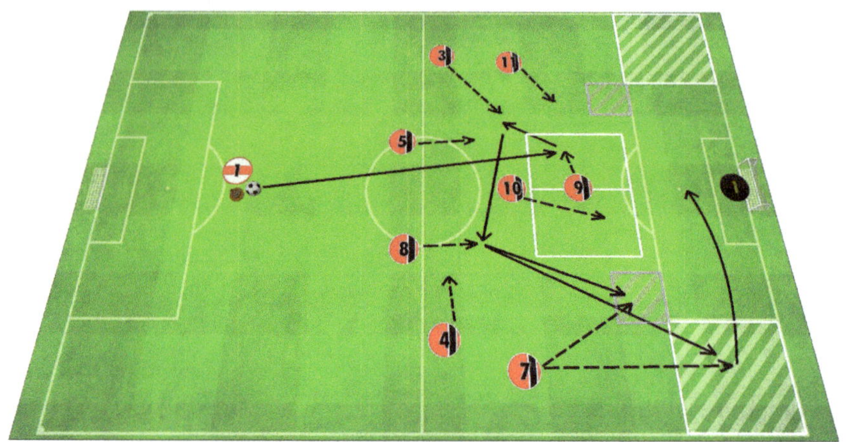

Description: this is a simulation of a 4-2-3-1 system. Start play from the goalkeeper with a pass to the area indicated by the movement of the center forward (9). The attacking midfielder (10) will move to the opposite area from the center forward. The fullback (3), the center midfielder (5) and the wing (11) will move towards the area where the center forward will control the ball in order to offer options. Once the number 9 can control the ball, he will give the ball to one of these three options (3, 5, and 11). The player receiving the ball will have to play quickly to the center midfielder (8) on the opposite side, who will play a pass to one of the zones marked out on the field, as indicated by the winger (7). Depending on the zone where the winger (7) receives the ball, he will have to shoot on goal or cross the ball into the penalty area.

A variation of this exercise is for the center forward to knock down the ball played from the goalkeeper for the attacking midfielder (10) to finish the move with a shot on goal.

B) Opposition - organization - second ball areas - finishing

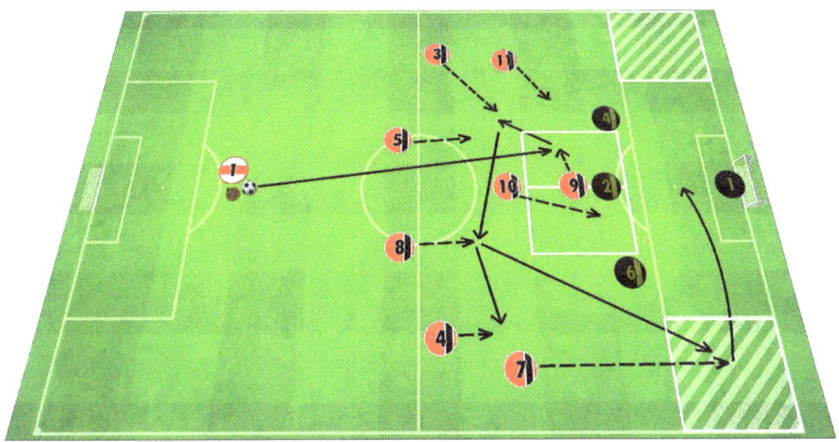

Description: the same as the previous exercise, with the addition of three opposing defenders who face the ball and wait for the long delivery from the goalkeeper. The beginning of the exercise is the same. The difference is that there will be a battle for the ball between the center forward (9) and the opposing centerback (2). To increase the difficulty we can add defensive help from the corresponding side (4 or 6), according to where the goalkeeper plays the ball. The play needs to be finished on the opposite side from where the center forward (9) and opponents battled for the ball.

C) Increased game realism

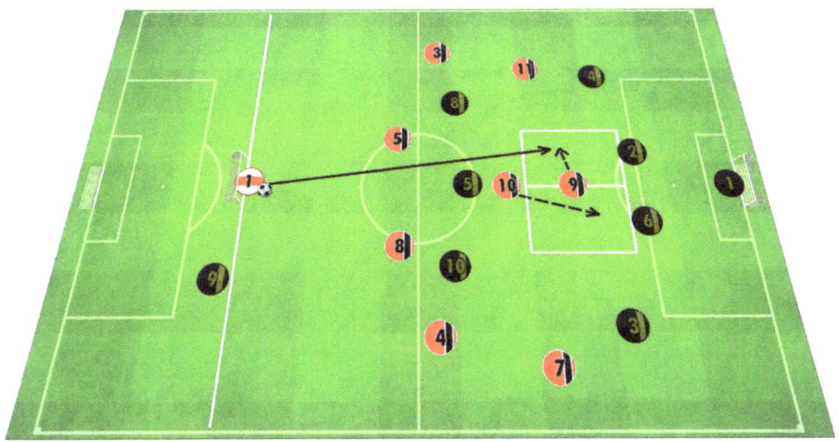

Description: organize the defending team in a line of four defenders, plus three center midfielders and a forward who waits behind the line where the goalkeeper starts with the ball. Start play in the same way as the previous exercise and with the same objective of winning the second ball and attacking. When the defending team recovers the ball, they counterattack with a pass into the forward who is waiting outside the line shown in the diagram so that they can play 8v8. In this way, the team that was originally attacking will have to train the concept of recovering the ball after losing it.

EXERCISES

PROGRESSION AND FINISHING

Exercises For Progression And Finishing

The objective of these exercises it to finish the play through a positional attack, by employing the specific tactical offensive concepts that have been analyzed in the game situations of each of these coaches.

Situations:

1. Playing between the lines.
2. Play short to attract and then play long.
3. Play quickly and vertically.
4. Playing through the wings.
5. Switch play.
6. Offensive disorder.
7. Resolving in your own style.

Exercises: Progression - Finishing

Training the situation: playing between the lines.

A) Unopposed - decision making - accuracy between the lines.

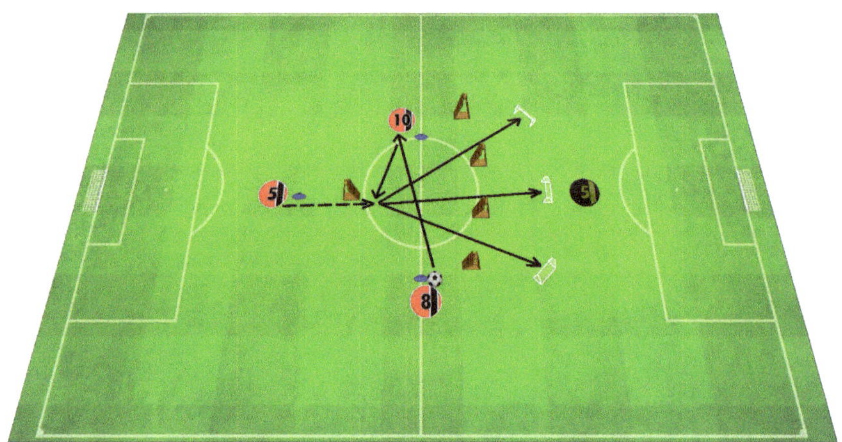

Description: 8 starts play by passing to 10, who dismarks and plays one touch to 5, who starts at the cone and receives ahead of the obstacle. At this moment, 5 controls the ball and has to score in any of the three mini goals. Then rotate positions. Play continuously, gradually increasing the speed of the passing. To add complexity and improve decision making, and an opposing defender between the obstacles and the mini goals who will try to intercept the passes into the goals.

B) Opposition - superiorities - accuracy between the lines - finishing.

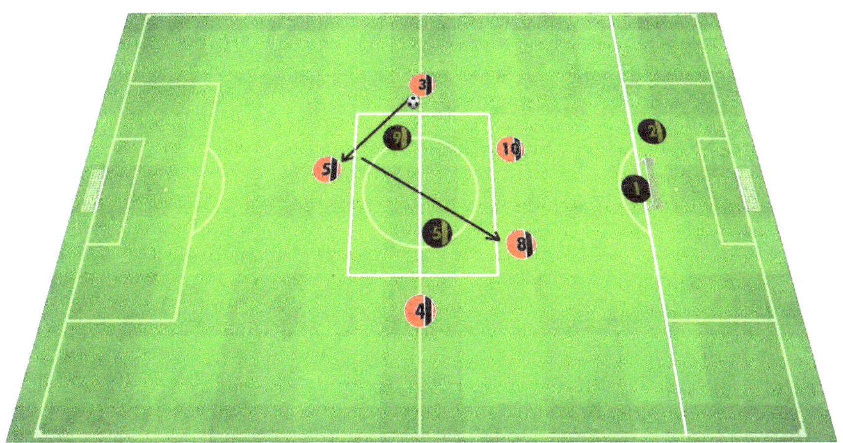

Description: play 5v2, with the attacking team taking up positions that simulate a 4-3-3. After a possession sequence of four consecutive passes, 8 or 10 may receive the ball from 5 with an oriented control and finish with a shot on goal.

To add complexity, add a defender (2) near the goal who is allowed to jump up with the pass to 8 or 10 in order to pressure and prevent a goal from being scored. The positioning can be adjusted to a 4-2-3-1 system by inverting the midfield triangle.

C) Increased game realism.

Description: play 11v9. The attacking team plays in a 4-3-3 formation

and the defending team plays in two lines of four. The midfield line plus the center forward of the defending team must recover the ball in the first zone indicated in the diagram, and cannot drop back into the second (finishing) zone. These rules will allow the attacking team to always play with a numerical superiority, to find passes between the lines, and to play vertically to finish the play.

Training the situation: play short to attract and then play long.

A) Unopposed - change of rhythm to change the zone.

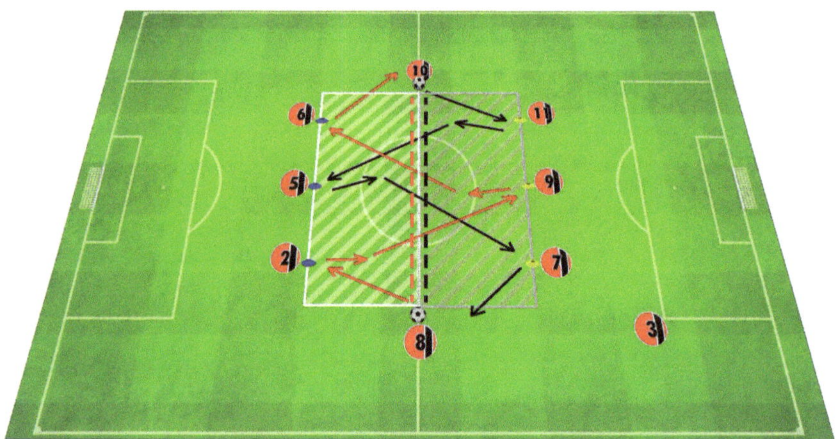

Description: 8 and 10 start at the same time, mirroring each other. Analyzing the 8, we see they start with a pass to 2, who returns it to 8. This player controls the ball with their far foot, the right, in order to pass with their left foot to 9. When this happens, 8 changes the speed of the run and looks to get the ball back from 9. This time 8 controls the ball with the left foot and plays the ball towards 6 with the right, again changing the speed of the run and looking to get the ball back from 6.

B) Opposition - possession - change of rhythm - change of zone.

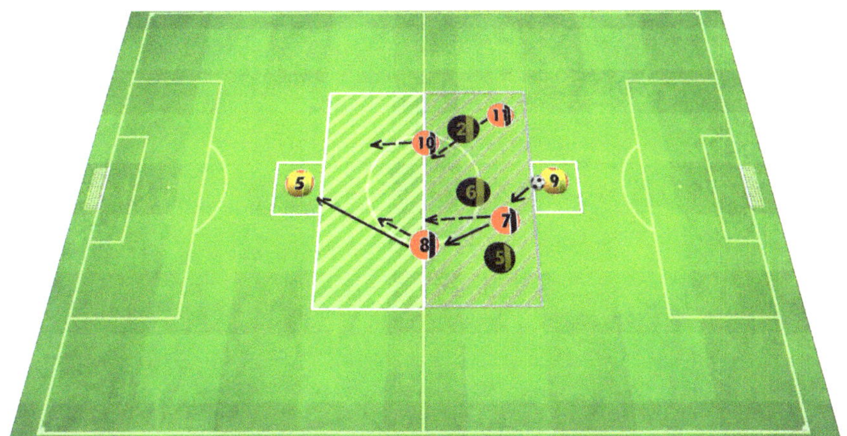

Play 5v3 on one half of the area marked out on the field. Players 10, 8, and 9 (who can only move within one of the smaller zones) who have possession of the ball, are fixed supports, while 11 and 7 play free within one half of the large zone. Players 5, 2, and 6 are the defenders.

After four consecutive short passes, the team in possession should move the ball to the other half of the large zone, through a pass on the ground to 5, who can only move within the small zone on the end.

C) Increased game realism.

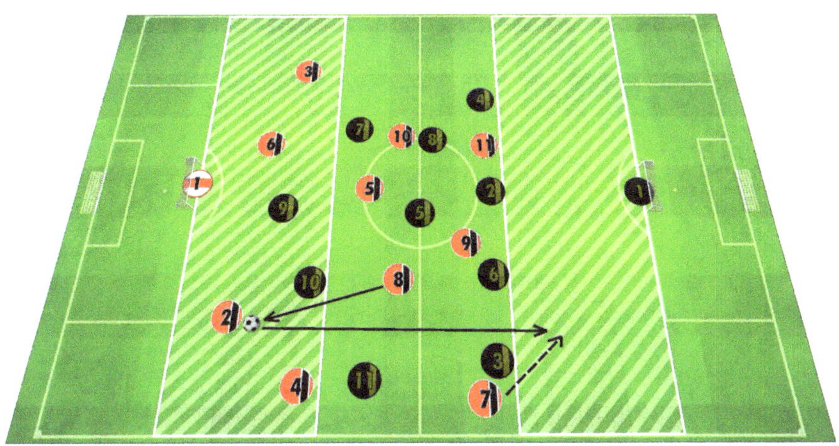

Description: play 11v11, both teams in 4-3-3 systems. The field is divided into three zones, but the teams will only play in two of them. This rule applies to both the attacking team and to the defending team trying to recover the ball. It's mandatory to play the ball on the ground, and the teams can only play from the central zone to the finishing zone with a long pass to a player who has previously dismarked.

Training the game situation: fast vertical play.

A) Different options - finishing in the mini goals.

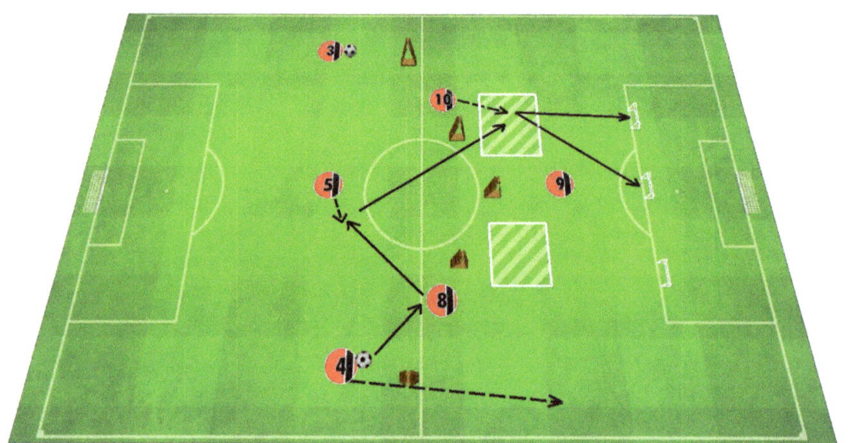

Description: start the circuit with two fullbacks (4 and 3) at the same time. In the diagram we can see two examples of starting the play with the right fullback (4).

Option 1: the right fullback (4) passes to the right center midfielder (8) and runs forward while the center midfielder (8) plays to the supporting defensive midfielder (5) who dismarks, controls the ball with the left foot, and then passes the ball between the lines to the left center midfielder (10) who shoots on one of the mini goals or sets up the center forward (9) to convert the goal.

Option 2: the right fullback (4) passes to the right center midfielder (8) and runs forward, while the right center midfielder (8) plays to the dismarking and supporting defensive midfielder (5), who controls the ball with the left foot and plays a deep pass to the center forward (9) after this player has dismarked. Finally, 9 scores into one of the mini goals or lays the ball off to one of the center midfielders (8 or 10) so that they can score. The option also exists for 9 to play to one of the fullbacks (4 or 3), so that one of these players can cross the ball to the center forward or one of the two center midfielders (8 or 10).

When you repeat the exercise, vary the number of passes, the passing options, the supports offered, and finish with different players.

B) Opposition - decision making - passes between the lines - finishing.

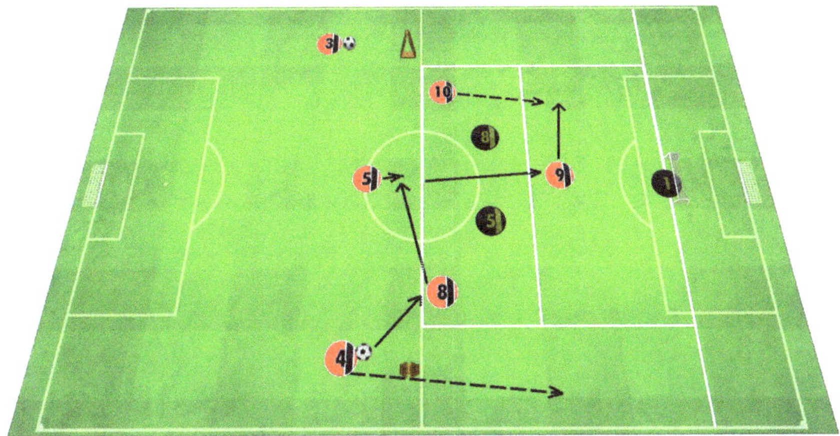

Description: put two opponents (5 and 8) inside the zone marked on the field. These opponents cannot leave their zone and must avoid being split by the pass. There is also a normal sized goal occupied by a goalkeeper (1).

The options for progression will be decided by the attacking players, always started by one of the fullbacks (4 and 3). The maximum number of passes before trying to play a pass between the defenders is three.

C) Increased game realism.

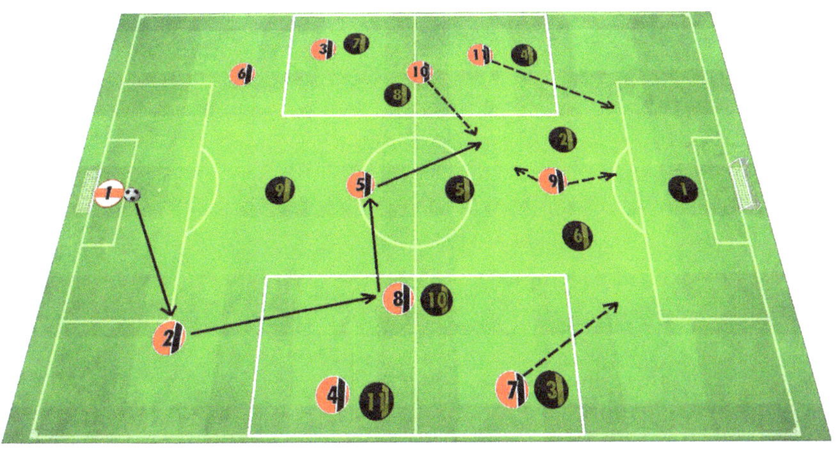

Play 11v11 with both teams in a 4-3-3 system. The goalkeeper (1) starts play to one of the two centerbacks (2 or 6). The goalkeeper and the two centerbacks need to eliminate the pressure of the opposing center forward (9), in order to be able to play into one of the two zones marked on the pitch, where they will be able to play with a numerical superiority (4v3).

There need to be at least two passes made within those zones before progressing into the finishing zone on the opposite side. There are always five players who participate in the finishing zone: right winger (7), right center midfielder (8), left center midfielder (10), left winger (11) and center forward (9).

Training the situation: playing through the wings.

A) Different options - finishing in the mini goal (by crossing the ball) – large goal (shooting on goal).

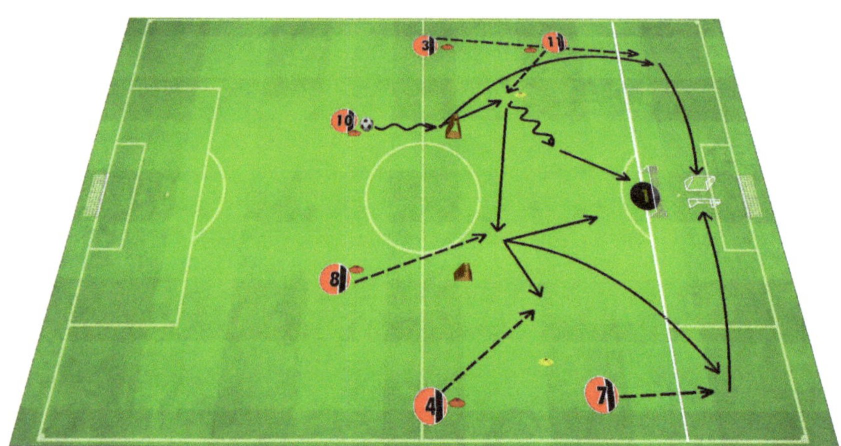

Description: start with the center midfielders (8 and 10). As an example, play starts with the left center midfielder (10) running with the ball towards the obstacle, in order to pass the ball to the left winger (11) who dismarks, dropping down to the inside, while the left fullback (3) attacks on the outside. The winger (11) carries out an oriented control after receiving the ball from the center midfielder (10), runs a little with the ball, and has three options:

Option 1: shoot on goal.

Option 2: pass into space towards the left fullback (3), simulating a 2v1.

Options 3: play the ball to the right center midfielder (8), who will decide how to finish the play.

The choices should vary, and it's recommended to repeat each option three or four times. The objective is to score in the goal with the fullbacks, center midfielders, and wingers, and also to look to place the balls in the mini goals through the fullbacks or wingers, simulating a cross on the ground.

B) Opposition - marked out zones - overlaps.

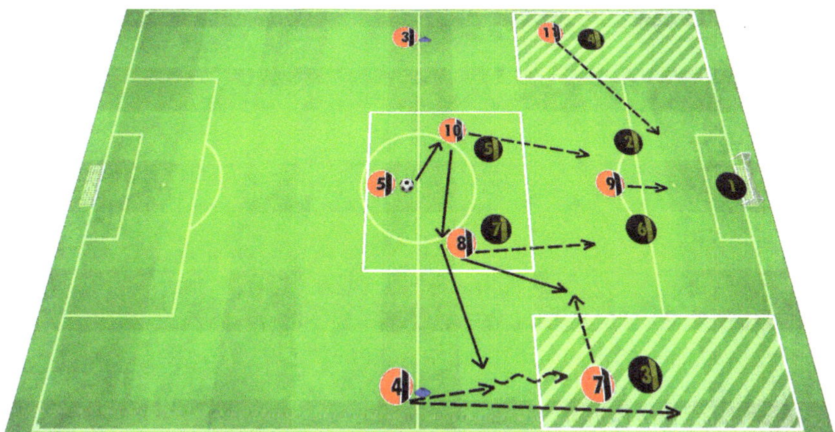

Description: start with a 3v2 inside the central zone marked out on the field. After a specific number of passes (or on the orders of the coach) play the ball towards one of the two fullbacks (4 or 3) so that these can play to the winger (7 or 11) and seek out a 1v1 against the opposing fullback. The other alternative is for the fullback in possession of the ball to pass to the winger, who dismarks inside to receive the ball outside the wide zone. In both situations the objective is to finish the play as quickly as possible.

C) Increased game realism.

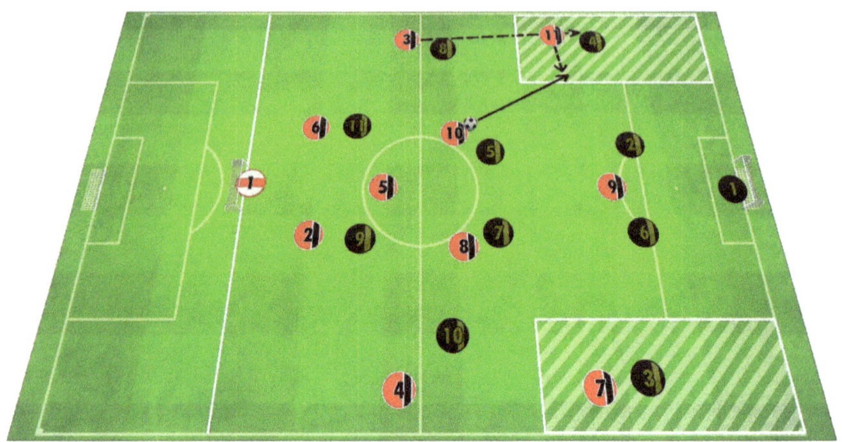

Description: play 11v11 with a 4-3-3 formation opposing a 4-4-2 formation. The only rule to be established is that only the opposing fullbacks (4 and 3) and wingers of the team in possession of the ball (7 and 11) can enter the wide zones. In this practice we are looking for superiorities on the wings.

Training the situation: offensive disorder.

A) Dismarking - different heights - passes.

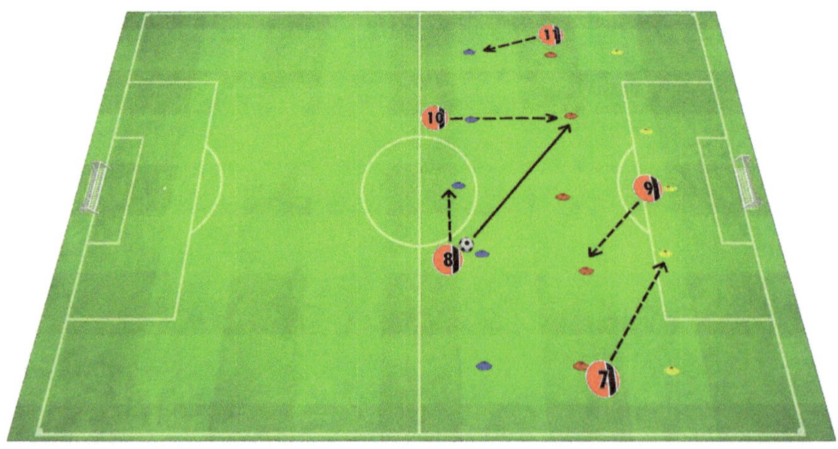

Description: mark out three rows of five cones, each row in a different color. These rows will show the different heights the players need to take up during the attack. Always try to have a rational distribution of space in the attack, both in width and in depth. The objective of this exercise is for the players to be in constant motion, giving passing options to the player who has the ball. These dismarkings will be towards the references provided by the colored cones and will take the team mates' movements into account. There needs to always be at least one player at each height; one on the line of blue cones, another on the red cones, and another on the yellow cones. The pass is made towards the cone indicated by the receiver. Each player needs to make a pass and the player with the ball decides where the ball should be played. After making a pass each player needs to move and occupy a different position. Once the pass is received, everyone moves again and indicates where the next pass to a different cone will be. The idea is that the players will be permanently changing positions.

B) Opposition - dismarking - 2 vs. 1 - finishing.

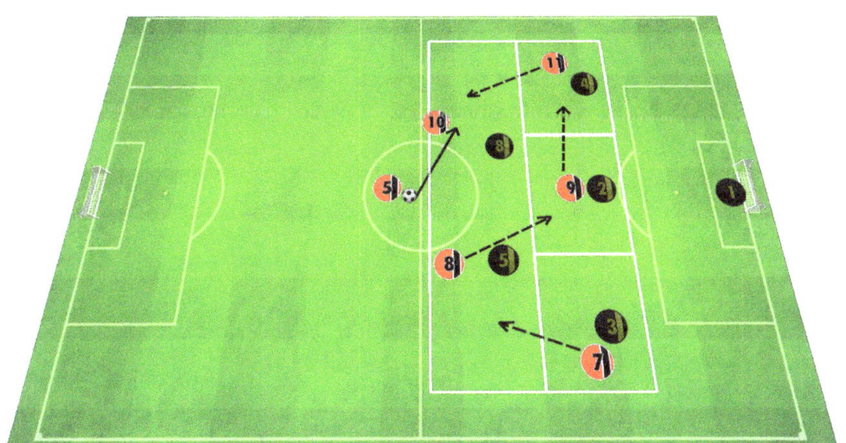

Description: set up a 6v5 game with different zones. Start play with the defensive midfielder (5) who plays outside the boundaries of the zones marked on the field, as a permanent support for the team in possession of the ball. The rule is that the attacking team must always occupy each zone with one of the five players that are inside the entire grid. The players move freely, but there cannot be more than two attacking players in the same zone, which produces, at most, a 2v1. The defensive midfielder (5) of the team in possession of the ball is the only player that the defending player cannot take the ball from. The objective is to find space, superiorities, and shots on goal to finish the play.

C) Increased game realism.

Description: play 11v11 with a 4-3-3 system playing against a 4-2-3-1. Play unlimited touches. The only rule is that the attacking team is obligated to occupy all of the channels when they are in possession with any of their players except for the two centerbacks (2 and 6) and the defensive midfielder (5).

Training the situation: switching play.

A) Alternating short and long passes - finishing.

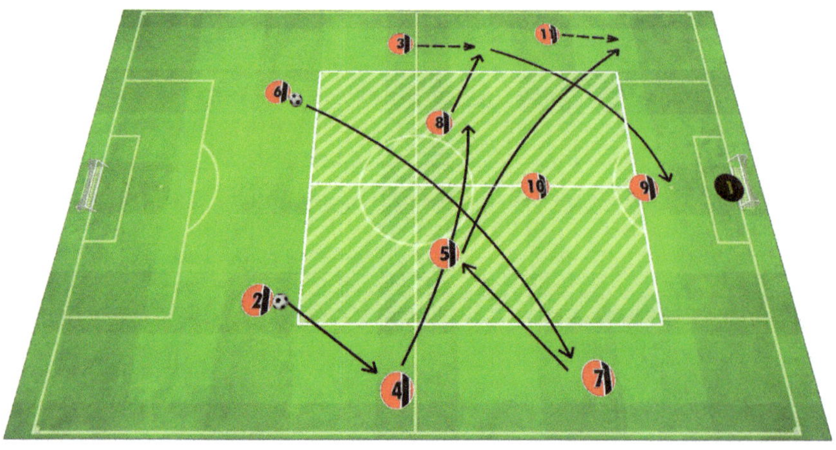

Description: start play from the two centerbacks. They will decide if they start with a short pass or a long pass. Then, according to the type of pass selected, the next pass needs to be the opposite of what the previous pass was. If a long pass is made first, the player will then make a short pass, and vice versa. The pass is considered long when it jumps one of the zones marked out on the field, and as a condition of the activity, the long passes need to always be in the air. In contrast, the short passes can be made backwards, to simulate a support to change the point of attack. Finishing needs to be preceded by a long pass.

B) Opposition - short - long - finishing.

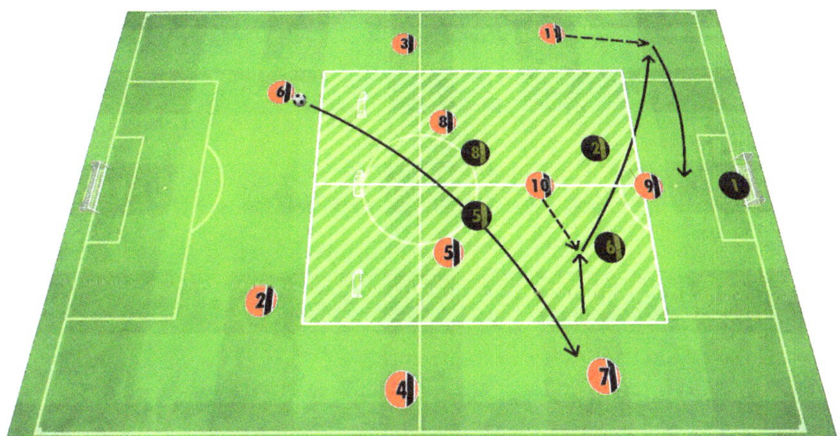

Description: start from the two centerbacks, following the same rules as the previous exercise, but now adding four opponents who are not allowed to leave the marked zone. If these players manage to cut off a pass, they must try to score immediately into the mini goals as quickly as possible. In this way, the team which was in possession is obliged to close down and pressure the opponents after losing the ball in order to prevent them from scoring.

C) Increased game realism.

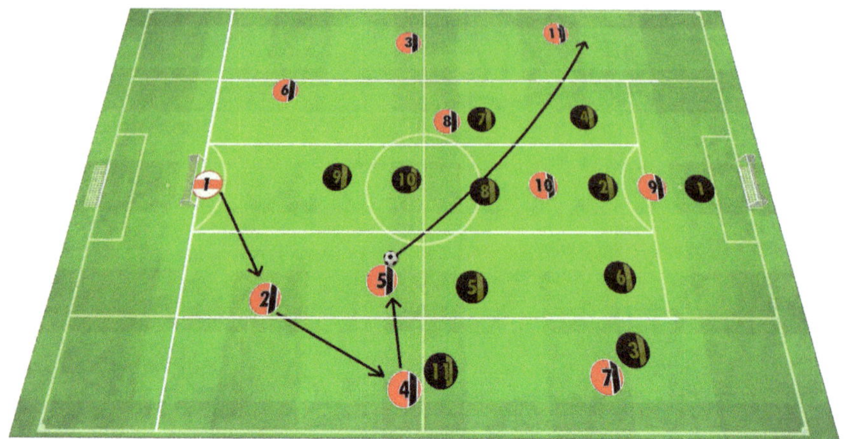

Description: play 11v11 with both teams playing in a 4-2-3-1 system. Divide the field into five channels. The only rule is that the team without the ball in the defensive phase must contract and occupy for of the lanes, which will encourage the team with the ball to switch play.

Training the situation: resolving in your own style.

A) Possession - opposition - numerical equality.

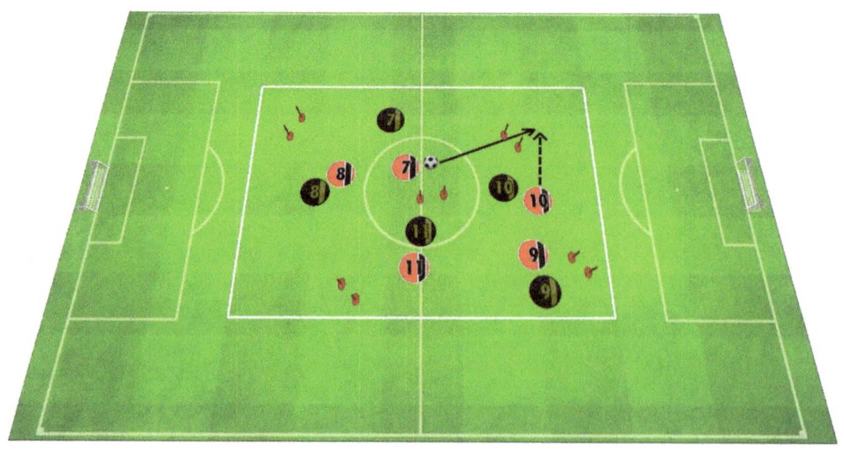

Description: play 5 v 5 with five mini goals marked out with poles. A goal is scored by running with the ball through one of the mini goals or when the ball is passed through the poles and received by a team mate on the other side. Two goal may not be scored consecutively in the same mini goal.

B) Positional Organization - opposition - duels - individual solutions

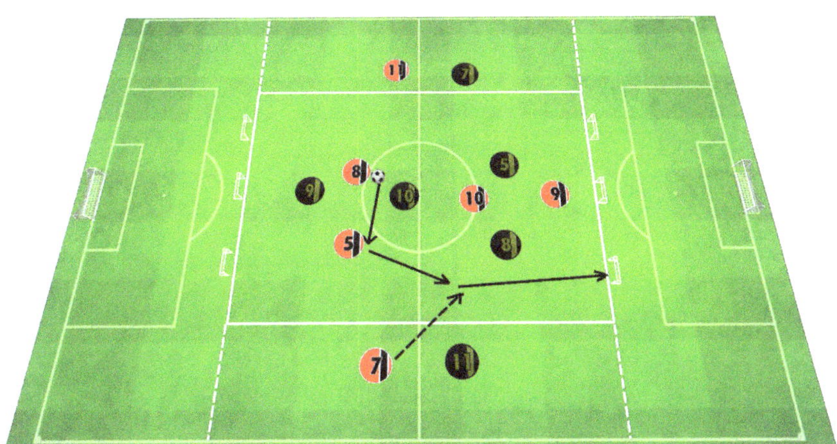

Description: play 6 v 6 on a field divided into zones. Play 4 v 4 in the central zone and 1 v 1 in the side zones, with the wingers of both teams facing each other. A goal is scored either by shooting into one of the three mini goals in the central zone, or by carrying the ball across the opponent's end line in either of the lateral zones.

C) Increased game realism.

Description: play 11 v 11 with two 4-2-3-1 systems facing each other.

Divide the field in zones with equal numbers, except in the finishing zone of both teams where there will be two centerbacks against one center forward. Play without a touch limitation. Players must respect their positions and may only join the finishing zone when it's time to finish off the attack. They can join that zone by combining with the center forward or by running into the zone with the ball. Once the player in possession has entered the final zone, they can only be marked by one of the two centerbacks (2 and 6).

The Coaches - By The Numbers

These statistics were taken from the 2018-2019 Premier League season, when these four coaches led their teams to the top four places in the league table: Manchester City (98 points), Liverpool (97 points), Chelsea (72 points), Tottenham (71 points).

In that same season Chelsea was UEFA Europa League champion while Manchester City, Tottenham, and Liverpool reached the semifinals of the Champions League. Klopp got his hands on that trophy after beating Spurs in the final.

As well as winning the Premier League, Guardiola also won the FA Cup that year (beating Watford 6-0 in the final).

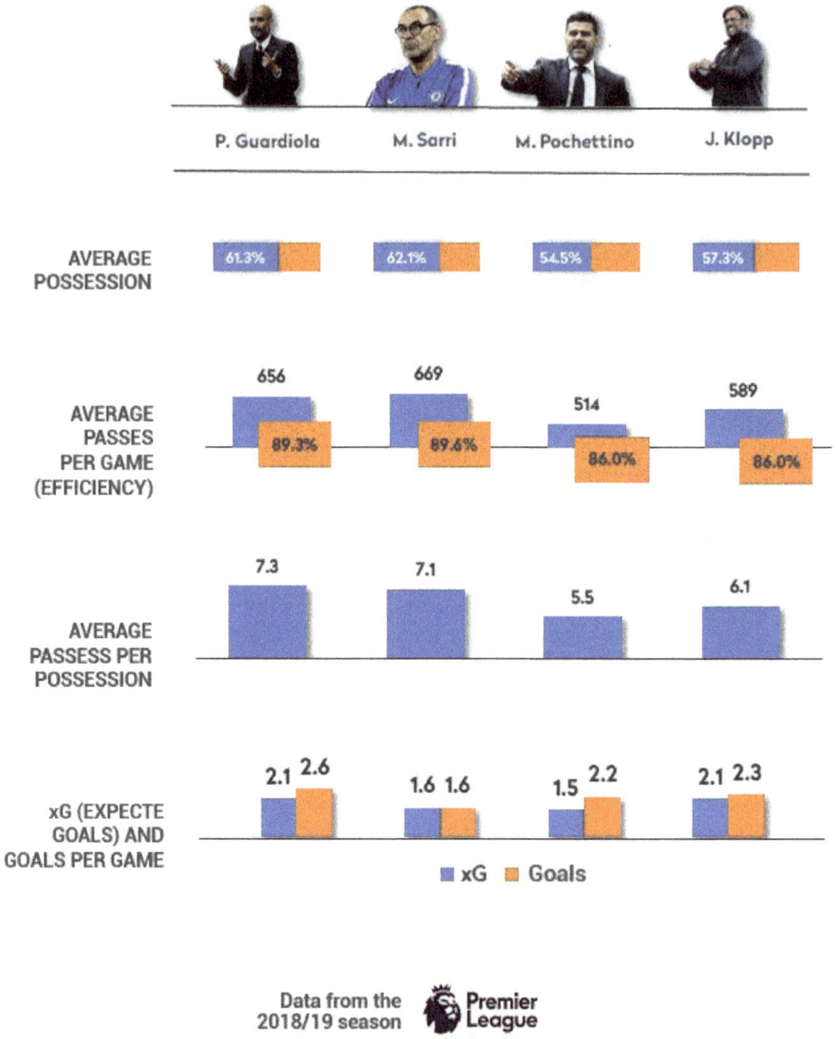

	P. Guardiola	M. Sarri	M. Pochettino	J. Klopp
AVERAGE POSSESSION	61.3%	62.1%	54.5%	57.3%
AVERAGE PASSES PER GAME (EFFICIENCY)	656 (89.3%)	669 (89.6%)	514 (86.0%)	589 (86.0%)
AVERAGE PASSESS PER POSSESSION	7.3	7.1	5.5	6.1
xG (EXPECTE GOALS) AND GOALS PER GAME	2.1 / 2.6	1.6 / 1.6	1.5 / 2.2	2.1 / 2.3

xG Goals

Data from the 2018/19 season Premier League

"Expected goals", also called xG, is a statistical indicator that assigns the probability of a goal to a scoring chance, according to the characteristics of the play. Not all scoring opportunities have the same probability of finding the net, and that probability depends on many factors: distance, angle, opponents in the way, etc.

ABOUT THE AUTOR

LUCAS RIVAS

Born in 1985 in Buenos Aires, Lucas Rivas is a professional football coach and a member of the Argentinian Association of Football Coaches (ATFA).

He started his career in Mexico in 2007, where was in charge of an affiliate team of Club Atlante in the Fourth Division Premier. At the same time he acted as the Sporting Director of the Mexican club's youth divisions.

The following year he started a long relationship with Argentina's Club Atlético Lanús. There, he was a staff member of the Coordinación General de Fútbol Juvenil and was an on-field assistant coach for Leandro Sime in the fourth division.

In 2011 he joined the first team staff as a Tactical Analyst for the first division. He worked in this capacity until 2015, becoming a specialist in Argentine soccer and winning the Copa Sudamericana in 2013 with Guillermo Barros Schelotto as head coach.

He also collaborated with Marcelo Bielsa's staff on the Chilean national team, where he created videos and reports about Chilean players who were playing with Argentinian teams.

Then in 2016, Ezequiel Carboni summoned him to become assistant coach for Lanús' second team ("Reserva"). A year later, in 2017, they took over the first division team. In 2018, they coached at Argentinos Juniors.

In 2019 he received a call from Javier Sanguinetti, who invited him to be part of his technical team as an on-field assistant for Club Sol America of Paraguay.

After this experience, in 2020, Rivas joined Nicolás Larcamón's technical staff at Chile's CD Provincial Curico Unido.

Later in 2020 he was once again at Sanguinetti's side; this time at Argentina's Banfield, where they had an excellent campaign and reached the final of the Copa Diego Maradona.

libro
futbol
.com
AL GOL SE
LLEGA LEYENDO

www.ingramcontent.com/pod-product-compliance
Ingram Content Group UK Ltd.
Pitfield, Milton Keynes, MK11 3LW, UK
UKHW062302290726
14090UKWH00017B/836